PITTSBURGH STEELERS
MEN OF STEEL

PITTSBURGH STEELERS
MEN OF STEEL

JIM WEXELL

SPORTS
PUBLISHING

Sports Publishing books may be purchased in bulk at special discounts for sales promotion, corporate gifts, fund-raising, or educational purposes. Special editions can also be created to specifications. For details, contact the Special Sales Department, Sports Publishing, 307 West 36th Street, 11th Floor, New York, NY 10018 or info@skyhorsepublishing.com.

Sports Publishing® is a registered trademark of Skyhorse Publishing, Inc.®, a Delaware corporation.

www.skyhorsepublishing.com

10 9 8 7 6 5 4 3 2 1

Library of Congress Cataloging-in-Publication Data

Wexell, Jim.
Pittsburgh Steelers : men of steel / Jim Wexell.
   p. cm.
ISBN 978-1-61321-047-5 (alk. paper)
1. Pittsburgh Steelers (Football team)--History. 2. Football players--Pennsylvania--Pittsburgh--History. I. Title.
GV956.P57W49 2011
796.332'6474886--dc22

                                        2011016604

Printed in the United States of America

This book is dedicated to and inspired by the short, brave life of Matthew Blake Cenkner.

CONTENTS

INTRODUCTION

My dad's first memory of Steelers football is of a night game at Forbes Field. The ball was white, and his favorite player, Ernie Stautner, had just been ejected without explanation. The big guy sitting a row in front began to laugh.

"What's so funny?" my dad asked.

The man turned around. It was boxing champ Billy Conn.

"Stautner," Conn said with a chortle. "He's wearing baseball spikes."

Ernie Stautner, the original Man of Steel, eventually became the first and, to this day, only player to have his jersey retired by the Pittsburgh Steelers. He played the defensive line for the Steelers from 1950 to 1963 and is remembered for his toughness, his quickness, and his forearm shiver.

Dick Hoak was asked, prior to Super Bowl XL, which player, in his 44 years with the Steelers, has been forgotten by time. He didn't bat an eye when he said Stautner.

"Everybody talks about Terry and Joe, who were great players," Hoak said. "But Ernie Stautner was a great, great football player. He's the only Steeler with his jersey retired. That's how much the organization, the Rooneys, thought of him."

Hoak came to the Steelers from Penn State in 1961. His thoughts on his playing days, and later his coaching days, are included in this book. They were gathered that day, four days before he won his fifth championship ring.

Among the crowd of reporters sitting at Hoak's table that media day were sportswriting giants Dave Anderson of the *New York Times* and Bob McGinn of the *Milwaukee Journal-Sentinel*. They could've chatted with Ken Whisenhunt or Dick LeBeau, or Jerome Bettis or Hines Ward, but they chose Hoak, an assistant coach, and they stayed with him throughout the allotted time reporters were given to speak with the team. But if Hoak is the voice of experience in the organization, Stautner is the godfather, the enduring spirit.

* * *

Stautner is not one of the 35 men profiled in this book. A world war and 14 seasons in the pits of professional football, not to mention 23 years spent trying to beat his old team as an assistant coach with the Dallas Cowboys, combined to exact a toll from Stautner, who suffered with Alzheimer's Disease for eight years before he died less than two weeks after the Steelers won their fifth world championship.

Stautner was the embodiment of a rough-and-tumble organization that's been ridiculed at times and placed on a pedestal at other times. Whether he was mashing running backs with metal spikes, leading the league's top-ranked defense or drinking shots with Bobby Layne, Stautner was a Steeler through and through. *Men of Steel* is a book that chronicles the history of this colorful organization through its players. It's a history that's told through those who lived it, and those men didn't have to win championships; they didn't have to win rushing titles; they didn't even have to use a forearm shiver to draw inclusion into this book. They only needed to be interesting, whether on the field or off, and that certainly allowed for a large pool from which to choose.

* * *

The old joke about the "Same Old Steelers" doesn't ring true for those who struggled with the ups and downs of an organization that has come to symbolize football excellence. Many of these players fought through the myth that the early days of the Steelers were days to be ridiculed.

"That just wasn't true," said team chairman Dan Rooney. "In every decade we had half-decent teams. In '36, they were really good. The '40s came and we really would've been OK. In '41 and '42, when Dudley was the first pick, we had good teams, but the war took them all. They came back and we got Jock in '46. In '47 we had a playoff game with the Eagles. That was the year we struck, and that created a real problem for us. The players were grousing, and Jock was really tough. He'd say, 'Don't give them anything,' and that kind of stuff. Then the early '50s were really good, and the early '60s were really good. That's when we got Buddy Parker as the coach.

"In '62 we were very good, and in '63 we tied all those games. We beat the Giants 31-0 the first time we played them but the next time they beat us in a close game. Cope loves to tell the story that they all went on the wagon and that's why we lost. And then of course came the '70s and '80s, and you know where we are now."

Don't sweat the details. They fill the following pages.

PITTSBURGH STEELERS
MEN OF STEEL

CHAPTER 1

Bill
Dudley

Bill Dudley was the last player to win an NFL rushing title as a member of the Pittsburgh Steelers, and after his playing days Dudley went on to become perhaps the last honest politician. Dudley entered the Virginia General Assembly as a conservative Democrat in 1966, and after his first term a friend said to him, "Bill, you're a damn good legislator, but a miserable politician."

"I considered that a compliment," Dudley said some 40 years later. "And he said, 'I meant it as a compliment, but I don't know how long you're going to be around.'

"I just called it like I saw it. That was my problem there in Pittsburgh."

In Pittsburgh in the 1940s, "Bullet" Bill Dudley was considered the greatest to ever play for the Steelers, but his time in town was brief. Dudley was the first pick of the 1942 draft out of the University of Virginia, where he set a national record with 134 points as a senior. He played with the Steelers that year, and then served two years in the Army Air Force before returning late in 1945. His final year in Pittsburgh was 1946, when a conflict with Coach Jock Sutherland led to Dudley being traded to the Detroit Lions.

Even though Dudley rushed for only 1,504 yards and passed for 948 in two-plus seasons as a left halfback in Pittsburgh's single-wing offense, he's considered the greatest Steeler of the pre-1970s era, because he probably saved the franchise when he came along in 1942. On his second pro carry, the small-but-slippery Dudley ran 44 yards for a touchdown, and in his second game he returned a kickoff 84 yards for a touchdown. Despite Dudley's efforts, the Steelers were 0-2 after those two games, and they were looking like the same old 1-9-1 team from the previous year. That's when Redskins owner George Marshall convinced a distraught Art Rooney to keep his franchise through the end of the season, but only so he could sell it for more money in the off-season.

PITTSBURGH STEELERS IMAGE LIBRARY

BILL DUDLEY
Seasons with Steelers: 1942, 1945-46
Position: halfback
Height: 5-foot-10
Playing weight: 182 pounds

Marshall also suggested the teams play their return game that season in Baltimore in order to attract a bigger crowd.

However, with Dudley leading the way, the Steelers won three games in a row for the first time in six seasons. At 3-2 they returned to Forbes Field for the return game with Sammy Baugh and the Redskins, and they were greeted by an overflow crowd of 35,176. It broke the previous team attendance record by more than 6,000 fans. The Steelers lost the game, 14-0, but it would be their only loss throughout October and November of that season. They won four of their final five games to finish 7-4, the first winning season in team history.

Dudley rushed for 696 yards to lead the league. He was named Rookie of the Year and finished second to Don Hutson in the voting for Most Valuable Player. He also played in the Pro Bowl and sparked the NFL All-Stars to a 17-14 win over the champion Redskins with a 97-yard interception return for a touchdown.

Dudley entered the service in February of 1943 and played for the Air Force's champion Randolph Field Flyers in 1944. He was named to the Associated Press All-Service Team, as were future NFL stars Otto Graham and Charlie Trippi. The Steelers, meanwhile, plummeted. Because they hadn't planned for the war-time manpower shortage, the team merged with the Philadelphia Eagles to form the Steagles in 1943. However, they were only called the Steagles in Pittsburgh. Philadelphia officials refused to acknowledge the merger and did away with the few Steelers on the roster at season's end.

In 1944, the Steelers merged with the Chicago Cardinals. A player revolt, caused by the fining of Dudley replacement Johnny Butler for "indifferent play," nearly ended the season after three games, but the Card-Pitts plodded on through an 0-10 season. Dudley returned to the 1-5 Steelers on November 11 of the following 1945 season and helped them defeat the Cardinals, 23-0. The Steelers finished 2-8, but help was on the way in the form of new coach Jock Sutherland, a local favorite whose 15-year coaching career at Pitt ended when he fought the school's de-emphasis of athletics.

Sutherland signed a five-year contract as not only the new Steelers coach, but also a vice president with an option to eventually buy out co-owner Bert Bell. Dudley hailed the hire, but came to dislike Sutherland, who made "sarcastic comments about Dudley's sidearm passing motion" during a preseason passing drill, according to the Pro Football Researchers Association. After Dudley then suggested that defensive players wear different color jerseys than offensive players in practice, "words were exchanged" in front of the rest of the squad. Sutherland later apologized, and Dudley forgave him, but he didn't forget.

"Playing for Art Rooney," as he differentiated at the time in spite of his new coach, Dudley led the NFL in rushing (604), interceptions (10), and punt return yardage (385) in 1946. The Steelers went 5-5-1 and set a team attendance record (35,365 per game). With three minutes left in the final game, Dudley tore knee ligaments, and the 175-pounder said he would retire. The Steelers didn't believe him until Dudley took a job as an assistant coach at Virginia. That's when the

Steelers traded Dudley and Jack Dugger to the Lions for three halfbacks and a 1948 first-round draft pick.

"I thoroughly enjoyed my time in Pittsburgh," Dudley said. "I'm sorry I couldn't have continued my whole career there. We played a good football game, got some good crowds in Pittsburgh, and I think the football we played kept the fans happy, both in '42 and '46."

Walt Kiesling coached the Steelers in 1942. "There was a helluva big difference between Coaches Sutherland and Kiesling," Dudley said. "Jock had been a very successful college coach, and he had certain ways he wanted to do things and it was going to be done that way."

Without Dudley in 1947, the Steelers made their first playoff appearance, but Dudley would haunt them. In the 1947 opener, won by the Steelers, Dudley scored all 10 points and intercepted a pass for the Lions. In 1948, he scored all 17 points and intercepted a pass in the final minute of a Lions win. In 1950, playing for the Redskins, Dudley intercepted two passes and returned a punt 96 yards for a touchdown. Dudley, who was elected to the Hall of Fame in 1966, retired after the 1953 season to became an assistant coach at Virginia for two years. He turned down an offer from Carroll Rosenbloom to become head coach of the Baltimore Colts in 1954.

"Carroll talked to me just before he hired Weeb Ewbank," Dudley said. "I knew Mr. Rosenbloom. I'd known him for some years. He asked me what kind of contract I wanted and I told him five years. He said, 'What about three?' I said, 'Carroll, I don't think it can be done in three years,' and I think it was five years before the Colts won a championship."

While the Colts were gearing up for title runs in 1958 and 1959, Dudley was back in Pittsburgh in 1956 coaching running backs. The Steelers brought in Buddy Parker to coach in 1957 and Dudley became a part-time scout with the Steelers and then the Lions.

"I would love to have coached," he said. "I'd have won. I never worried about that. But to be a successful coach you had to be willing to move your family, and I wasn't willing to move. And in 1950 my older brother had come to me—he was in the life insurance business—and he offered to top what anyone else would pay me, so I went to work in the life insurance business and really only finally retired this past year."

Dudley was an estate planner for The Equitable throughout the majority of his post-playing days. He quit for good in 2005 at the age of 83. He still lives in Lynchburg, Virginia, with Libba, his wife since 1947. They have three children—Jarrett, Becca, and Jim—and four grandchildren.

As for his political career, Dudley said: "I went in as a Democrat, but then I switched parties when Nixon got ice-boxed. The Democratic Party just got too liberal for me, and so I was defeated when Nixon got caught with his hands in the cookie jar that fall. But that didn't bother me. I knew it was about time for me to get out. There were changes being made. And like I said, I couldn't go along with the changes in the Democratic Party at all."

Dudley's most significant piece of legislation increased the driver's age in Virginia from 14 to 16. "I was told it didn't stand a chance because it had been put in two or three times before and one fellow was against it," Dudley said. "So I went to see him. He became a very good friend of mine. He was from the rural area of Virginia, a very fine man. He said farm boys shouldn't have to have a driver's license to drive a tractor. I said they don't on the fields, but when they get on highways they do. I said that's just the way it ought to be. Statistics proved it: People 14 and under and older people caused most accidents. It passed my first year in the legislature."

In retirement, Dudley is a golfer and card player and passionate follower of Virginia football. He was pleased in April of 2005 that his Steelers made Heath Miller their first first-round pick from Virginia since they chose Dudley in 1942. Miller and Dudley both grew up in western Virginia coal towns situated about 40 miles apart.

Dudley still attends at least one Steelers game a year. "I'm very, very fond of Pittsburgh," he said. "Pittsburgh's been good to Bill Dudley, and I like to think that I tried to reciprocate. It's where I like to be remembered as playing ball. Nothing against Washington or Detroit, it was just my first stop, and I became friends with Mr. Rooney. He was an employer who later turned into a very good friend. I think Pittsburgh's lucky to have somebody like the Rooney family involved in sports, in my opinion."

CHAPTER 2

Elbie Nickel

Elbie Nickel built his house in Chillicothe, Ohio, for $2,000 in 1949. He sold it for 60 times that amount in 2004. The buyers, after winning a brief but furious bidding war, were pleased. They may have known Elbie Nickel was once a star football player at Chillicothe High School, the University of Cincinnati, and the Pittsburgh Steelers, but more important to them was the fact Nickel ran one of the best-known construction companies in southern Ohio.

"Everybody in Chillicothe knows who he is," said Nickel's son Joe Nickel. "The people that I talked to, the lady that bought the house, they all talked about the fact that they knew, because of the construction company, that the house was well-constructed. They never mentioned the Steeler connection."

The fact that the greatest tight end in Steelers history is better known for his off-season job says that either A.) Nickel was one fine builder, or B.) Pro sport in the 1950s wasn't the game it is today. Both are true. When Nickel retired from the Steelers, it was to comply with his father's wishes to take over the construction business. So at the age of 35, Nickel got on with his life's work.

Nickel actually retired twice from the Steelers. At Forbes Field, for the final home game of the 1956 season, Nickel was honored beforehand and scored two touchdowns. He was carried off the field by teammates after the Steelers beat the Los Angeles Rams, 30-13. After the season, Nickel played in his third Pro Bowl and was named the Steelers' Most Valuable Player by the Curbstone Coaches of Pittsburgh. They presented him with a trophy engraved N-I-C-H-E-L. The slight didn't stop Nickel from coming back for one more season. New backfield coach Jim Finks persuaded Nickel to return in 1957. He caught only 10 passes, but in his second goodbye at Forbes Field he dove to catch a 6-yard fourth-quarter touchdown pass from Earl Morrall to clinch a 21-10 win over the New York Giants.

In the road finale two weeks later, Nickel caught four passes for 44 yards and finished his career as the Steelers' all-time leading receiver with 329 catches. He also retired as the league's Iron Man, having played in a then-NFL record 124 consecutive games. An arm injury in 1957 forced Nickel to miss the fifth game that season, which ended the streak.

What does he remember about playing pro football? "Well, very little," the 83-year-old said in 2005 from his room in an upscale Cincinnati nursing home.

Nickel played baseball and basketball at the University of Cincinnati, but he excelled on the gridiron. In 1942 he led the Bearcats to an 8-2 record, and in 1946, after serving in the military, captained the team to a 9-2 mark, its best in 49 years. Nickel scored the winning touchdown in a 15-6 opening-day win over defending Big 10 champion Indiana in what was the school's biggest victory of the pre-Sid Gillman era. Nickel signed a baseball contract with the Cincinnati Reds the following spring but the Steelers convinced him to play football after drafting him in the 15th round in 1947. He would go on to serve as their offensive captain from 1949 through 1957.

The 6-foot-1, 196-pound Nickel was primarily a blocker in the Jock Sutherland/John Michelosen single-wing offense before becoming a receiving threat in 1949, when he averaged 24.3 yards per each of his 26 catches. In the penultimate game of the 1949 season, Nickel caught seven passes for 192 yards against the Bears. He also suggested to Michelosen that the Steelers fake a punt from their own 3-yard line. Bobby Gage took the snap from the back of the end zone and ran for a 97-yard touchdown, the longest play in franchise history.

Nickel blossomed at tight end when Joe Bach brought the T-formation to Pittsburgh in 1952. Nickel was third in the NFL that season with 55 catches for 884 yards and nine touchdowns, all team records at the time. His best pro game occurred late that season. Against the Dick 'Night Train' Lane-led secondary of the Los Angeles Rams, Nickel caught 10 passes for 202 yards.

"We had a picture in the basement and we'd talk about it all the time," said Joe Nickel. "He was catching a pass over "Night Train" Lane. He had him beat by three or four steps."

In 1953, Nickel broke his own single-season team record with 62 catches. The mark stood until Roy Jefferson caught 67 passes for the Steelers in 1969. Nickel made the Pro Bowl after both the '52 and '53 seasons. He tailed off to 40 catches in 1954, but made what Dan Rooney called "the most famous play we had until the Immaculate Reception" in front of a standing-room-only crowd at Forbes Field. The play is stitched into Steelers lore as an X-and-O tapestry hanging in the South Side office building. It tells the story of the play-action

ELBIE NICKEL
Seasons with Steelers: 1947-57
Position: tight end
Height: 6-foot-1
Playing weight: 196 pounds

bomb from Finks to Nickel that sealed the win and gave the Steelers a 4-1 record in 1954. They stumbled after that game and finished 5-7 on the season.

Nickel caught 36 passes in 1955 and moved to halfback in 1956 before calling it quits after 1957. His 329 catches are 127 more than any other Steelers tight end. Bennie Cunningham is second with 202. The man they called "Elbows" was named the Steelers' all-time tight end when the 50th anniversary team was chosen in 1982.

The best memories? "I remember him flipping me a game ball after they beat the Browns one time," said Joe Nickel. "About the only other thing I remember is all that stuff they gave him at one of those farewell games. There's a picture in his scrapbook of the ceremony. I looked down at the recliner they gave him. It was his favorite chair until we got rid of it last year."

In 2005, Joe Nickel went through his 26th year as the athletic director at North College Hill High School in Cincinnati. It's the school made famous by basketball phenom O.J. Mayo, who at the time was considered the best prep player since LeBron James. Joe Nickel was something of a prep phenom himself. He followed in his father's football footsteps at Chillicothe High and Cincinnati.

"I always wanted to be able to outrun him," he said of his dad. "Every year, every spring, we'd have our charge across the front yard to see if I could outrun him. I think I was 17 years old and he was about 42 before I could finally outrun him, and one of the things I could do was run. I was fourth in the state track meet my senior year in the 100 and 200, but I had to wait that long to outrun him in the 30-yard dash because he could move."

Nickel also remembers his dad calling Art Rooney "a father-like figure." The Chief, in fact, named one of his Maryland-bred race horses "Elbie Nickel." Every spring Elbie drove to the Louisville airport to meet the Chief and escort him to the Kentucky Derby.

"It went on for 20, 30 years," Joe Nickel said. "The funny thing was he'd always bring back a mint julep glass for my mom. And then I got married and he wound up having to bring back two mint julep glasses. And then my sister said, 'Where's mine?' And my dad said, 'I can't drink them. I don't like those drinks, those mint julep drinks. I can't drink three of them.' I don't know what he did but he showed up a couple of times with three glasses. We've got a whole set of Kentucky Derby glasses, had them for 20 or 25 years."

Elbie still receives attention from autograph seekers. One was a vice-president with the Green Bay Packers. In 1999, he wrote to ask for an autographed picture for his grandson. Nickel obliged and received a promise from the VP that was repaid to Nickel's grandson.

"My son Mike moved to Milwaukee and my dad gave him the guy's number and said, 'Call him up. He'll get you two tickets to a Packers game,'" Joe Nickel said. "So my son called the guy up and he said okay. My son went into work—he'd only been in Milwaukee for a year—and he told the guys he was going to the Packers' game. They all laughed at him and said, 'Yeah, right. You can't get into that game. Those tickets are gone.' So he reached into his pocket and showed them tickets in row eight. They were all stunned."

After Nickel retired from football, he joined the Butt Construction Company, so named after co-founder Jim Butt. With his father (Joseph Richard Nickel), brother (Eugene Nickel), and Butt, Elbie Nickel's crew built all of the Kroger, Big Bear, and K-Mart stores from Cincinnati to Huntington, West Virginia.

"Construction really boomed in this country after the war and they really took off," Joe Nickel said. His dad worked full-time until the age of 60, but Elbie didn't stop working. He helped friends and family in Chillicothe and served as the handy man at the local Trinity United Methodist Church.

"In Chillicothe they actually built a shopping center, or more of a strip mall, called Central Center. My grandfather and my dad had a lot of stock in that, and it's still right there."

So, Elbie struck it rich after football?

"Oh yeah, my grandfather and my dad, they were well off. He's well taken care of."

CHAPTER 3

Lynn Chandnois

Gale Sayers holds the NFL record for highest career kickoff return average. Sayers averaged 30.56 yards per return. Second on the all-time list is Lynn Chandnois, who played for the Steelers from 1950 to 1956. Chandnois averaged 29.57 per return.

Had Chandnois been credited with the 97-yarder that was waved off to open the 63-7 route of the New York Giants in 1952, he ... well, he wouldn't have been able to return the do-over 91 yards for a real touchdown. That improbable feat happened on November 30 in a game that's still considered one of the Steelers' greatest wins.

Chandnois was a fleet halfback selected with the eighth pick of the 1950 draft out of Michigan State. He led the league in kickoff returns in 1951 and was leading the pack in 1952 when he lined up to receive the opening kickoff against the powerful Giants. The Steelers entered that season with high hopes. New coach Joe Bach brought them out of the dark ages with the installation of the T-formation, but five losses by a total of 17 points left them with a disappointing 3-6 record as they hosted the 6-3 Giants, who were tied for first place in the Eastern Conference.

The first snow of winter had fallen the previous night and the shivering crowd was estimated at 5,000 when the Giants won the toss and elected to kickoff. By the end of the game, due in part to Chandnois' exploits and the wonders of radio, the crowd had grown to 15,000.

Chandnois took the opening kick at his 3-yard line and returned it for a touchdown, but it was called back because of an offsides penalty. As Chandnois awaited the re-kick, he met official Lloyd Brazil, who'd been a prep star in their hometown of Flint, Michigan.

"We chatted a bit and he said, 'Let's see you take this one back, too,'" remembered Chandnois. "So I did. I took it all the way back and he was down

11

LYNN CHANDNOIS
Seasons with Steelers: 1950-56
Position: running back
Height: 6-foot-2
Playing weight: 198 pounds

there in the end zone waiting for me. Obviously, he didn't take the same route I did to get there."

The double-dip sparked the Steelers to a 63-7 win over the Giants, who scored their only touchdown on a 70-yard flea-flicker pass by defensive back-turned-emergency quarterback Tom Landry. The upset knocked the Giants out of the race, and also cost their coach, Steve Owens, a book deal.

"He was going to publish a book on the umbrella defense," Chandnois said of what begat the standard 4-3 alignment. "I don't think he came out with it after that."

Chandnois finished the season with a league-leading kickoff-return average of 35.2, which remains a team record. His trick of the trade? "I'd use that pitcher's mound at Forbes Field to catch the ball on the run," he said. "It gave me an advantage and I'd use that mound to get a head start, to go downhill. I'd holler go and we did really well. Most of the guys now wait for the ball. They never catch it on the run. You've got to time that. You've got to sit back five yards and catch it on the run in full gallop. They don't teach that anymore."

After the game, assistant coach Walt Kiesling approached Rooney and said, "Isn't Chandnois the luckiest guy you ever saw in your life?"

Rooney relayed the story to Chandnois, who had a good laugh.

"I guess I was lucky both times," he said. "That was one of Art's favorite jokes."

Kiesling had the last laugh, though, when he became head coach in 1954. His first draft pick, Johnny Lattner, was made with replacing Chandnois in mind. Chandnois, like a generation of Steelers fans to follow, saw Kiesling as a buffoon.

"We had a good team," Chandnois said. "But I never cared much for Kiesling. I never liked him. I was very disappointed when Joe Bach came down ill and he had to be replaced by Kiesling. I felt like walking out of training camp at the time when I heard that."

Kiesling, of course, cut John Unitas without giving him a chance in an exhibition game. Chandnois had a theory as to why Rooney kept Kiesling around.

"Art was into gambling and betting the horses and so forth, and I think that Walt Kiesling was quite a gambler too, and I think he lost, and I think that's the only way Art could get his money back was to hire him as the head football coach. Here's a guy who didn't know anything about the T-formation; he was a single-wing coach. And he'd only talk to certain players. He never talked to me."

Chandnois was the team's player rep at a time when players were fighting for their first pension plan. The first NFLPA boss, Creighton Miller, called Chandnois to see if he could meet the Steelers at training camp at St. Bonaventure. Kiesling turned Chandnois down, so Chandnois went to Rooney, who allowed it.

"Kiesling found out I went over his head and he never liked that," Chandnois said. "He was a hard man to get along with. Nobody really cared for him, but we couldn't do anything about it because he was a buddy of Art Rooney's. I tell you, it's hard to play for a coach you don't like, especially when you don't get paid much money. If we got paid the kind of money they're making today it'd be different."

Chandnois was a record-setting back at Michigan State. He still holds school records for average yards per rush in a season (7.5), career interceptions (20) and longest touchdown run (90). He often told his Steelers teammates that he'd taken a pay cut when he left college ball. Chandnois once had to call his old coach, Biggie Munn, to send his old equipment because the Steelers' equipment was so beat up.

"We'd have two-and-a-half-hour practices in the morning and in the afternoon, and you only had one change of clothes: one jock, one T-shirt and one pair of socks. We'd go out in the morning and come back in the afternoon and they were just wringing wet. We had to lay them out in the sun to let them dry for afternoon practice. A lot of times they weren't dry and you'd get jockstrap itch and everything else. So I went up to Kiesling and asked about getting a new set of clothes for the second practice. He said he'd see what he could do. Well, he came back and said we're going to change: You change with Butler; Butler you change with Mathews; and so on. That didn't go over too good."

Kiesling worked the Steelers hard through the two-a-days and he played the first team throughout most of the six-game exhibition season. The numbers show that Kiesling's teams started fast but ran out of gas. The Steelers started 4-1 in both 1954 and 1955 and won only one game combined in the final seven games of each season. In 1956, the Steelers started slow and finished 5-7. It marked the end for both Kiesling and Chandnois.

"Of course, Buddy Parker kept him as an assistant, too, and why he did I'll never know. Of course, Buddy was a party coach anyway."

Chandnois had been in and out of the Steelers' lineup with injuries in 1954 and 1955, and he suffered a career-ending shoulder injury midway through the 1956 season in Cleveland. Chandnois came back to training camp the next season, but Parker, the new coach, told him he'd be released if the shoulder hadn't healed. "And that's when I hung it up," Chandnois said.

Aside from his gaudy kick-return stats, Chandnois finished his seven-year career with two Pro Bowl appearances, 1,934 rushing yards (3.3 avg.), 163 receptions (12.7 avg.), 285 passing yards and 162 points scored. It wasn't a bad output for someone prized for his blocking ability coming out of college.

After football, Chandnois and Pirates pitcher Bob Friend sold mutual funds together, but Chandnois sold his share of the business to begin work as a sales manager for Jessup Steel in Detroit, where he worked for 30 years. Chandnois lives just outside of Flint with his wife Paulette, whom he'd met in Uniontown, Pennsylvania. He has two daughters, Suzanne and Lynda.

"I went back to watch practice one time in Pittsburgh," Chandnois said. "We walked out there at Three Rivers Stadium, and half the guys were lying down, relaxing. They never practiced together until maybe five minutes after everybody went in. That was under Noll. It sure was different than when I played."

Someone once said of Chandnois that if he'd played for Chuck Noll, he would've ended up in the Hall of Fame.

"I'd have to believe that," Chandnois said. "If I'd played for a good coach, yes."

CHAPTER 4

Jack Butler

One of the greatest defensive backs in NFL history always wanted to be a wide receiver. So every chance he could, in the summer of 1955, Jack Butler ran patterns for a scrub rookie quarterback named John Unitas.

"He was accurate. Man, he really was," said Butler. "But have you ever watched him? He was kind of awkward. There was something about him, kind of a little awkward and stiff, but, aw, man, he could throw the ball. He just never got much of a chance."

Butler was preparing for his fifth pro season with the Steelers at the time, while Unitas was in the midst of a training camp in which—the Associated Press reported that September—he threw only 30 passes in practice scrimmages, but connected for three touchdowns. Unitas wasn't receiving much of a chance from Coach Walt Kiesling and complained to Butler about it as the two drove from Pittsburgh to Olean, New York, for the resumption of camp at St. Bonaventure.

"We're driving back," Butler remembered, "and he said, 'I think they're going to cut me.' I said no, they have to give you a better look. He said, 'Oh, I don't know.' But we get up there for dinner, and we're walking back over, and Kies calls him over and cut him on the spot. It wasn't handled very well."

Unitas, of course, went on to become one of the game's greatest quarterbacks. Butler might've been so considered had Unitas remained in Pittsburgh to give the Steelers the offensive punch they lacked. As it stands, Butler is the best player from the 1950s who's not in the Pro Football Hall of Fame. He played cornerback and later safety for the Steelers from 1951 to 1959 and intercepted 52 passes during those 12-game seasons. His total is second in team history to Mel Blount's 57. Butler once intercepted an NFL and team-record four passes in a game against the Washington Redskins in 1953, and in the 1957 season Butler intercepted 10 passes. The Steelers led the NFL in total defense that year, as they did in 1958, but managed only third-place Eastern Conference finishes each season.

JACK BUTLER
Seasons with Steelers: 1951-59
Position: cornerback
Height: 6-foot-1
Playing weight: 200 pounds

"We always had a decent defense," Butler said. "But we never scored too many points."

Butler was named to the All-Decade Team by members of the Hall of Fame Selection Committee. Of the 23 players on that team, 21 are in the Hall of Fame. Butler and guard Dick Stanfel are the only exclusions. Butler, unlike Stanfel, has never even been a finalist. The slight has perturbed football people in Pittsburgh for a long time.

"They should give us the reason why he's *not* in the Hall of Fame," Art Rooney Jr. once said. Rooney was the personnel man behind the great Steelers teams of the 1970s.

"Jim Finks once told me that Jack Butler was one of the greatest athletes he had ever seen," Rooney said. "As you might know, Jim was a pretty good talent evaluator."

Butler also became a top-notch talent evaluator. He was installed as the head of LESTO (Lions, Eagles and Steelers Talent Organization) in the mid-1960s. When the Bears joined a few years later, it became known by its current name of BLESTO. Butler has remained the hub of the information co-op ever since. In 2005 it serviced nine teams, down from a high of 14 a few years earlier.

During that time, Butler tutored such personnel notables as Dick Haley, Tom Donahoe, Jack Bushofsky, Tom Modrak, Ron Hughes, and Kevin Colbert. In fact, Butler's son Mike helped build today's Indianapolis Colts into a powerhouse as their director of college scouting.

"The original people who really put BLESTO together were Buddy Parker and Art Rooney Jr.," Butler said. "Football was just starting to come alive. TV was becoming involved and it was getting bigger and nobody really had personnel departments. When I was playing in Pittsburgh, the man in charge of personnel was an undertaker on the North Side. He'd come around toward the end of the season and ask each guy if there were any good players at their old schools. He was a funeral director and I don't think he ever went out on the road. I don't think anybody did then except the Los Angeles Rams.

"In the early days we'd meet in say, Philadelphia or Detroit or here in Pittsburgh, and the day of the draft those BLESTO teams would come there and draft. At one time it was very, very important. Today, BLESTO's more of a starting point."

Butler's office in downtown Pittsburgh is the hub of BLESTO's information exchange. The member scouts send information on diskettes, and Butler updates his data base and e-mails teams to keep them up to date.

"The information is constantly coming in and going out for teams," Butler said. "We send all the information, the upgrades, downgrades. It's a full day."

Technology hasn't changed that. Butler used to spend full days writing up individual reports on NCR paper.

"Way back when, you'd write these things up, and you'd have to guess on the speed, or just say he's fast. Well, how the hell fast is he? Or I think he's 6-foot-2. But now it's so much more sophisticated."

Butler grew up in the nearby suburb of Whitehall. He didn't play high-school football and went off to St. Bonaventure, with Pirates slugger Frank Thomas, to join the priesthood. There Butler roomed with three football players who "jagged me into coming out" for the team. But Butler was turned away by the equipment manager, until the Chief's brother, Father Silas (Dan Rooney), intervened. He had played with Butler's dad and figured the kid was worth a shot. He was right. Butler set a conference record for receptions as a senior in 1950.

Butler wasn't drafted by the NFL, so he tried out for the Steelers the following summer at St. Bonaventure and found himself in a battle for the last roster spot with a former Pitt player. Coach John Michelosen, formerly the coach at Pitt, favored the ex-Panther, but that player was drafted into the service and Butler, who'd supported his mother and received a deferment, made the 1951 team as a 170-pound defensive end.

"I didn't play defensive back until someone got hurt in about the third game or so," he said. "I'll tell you one thing: No one got behind me that game. I was so far back no one could. That was the best thing that ever happened to me."

Butler became a starting cornerback and didn't miss a snap throughout the next eight seasons. An injured ankle in 1959 ended the iron-man streak. He came back for a game and then blew out his knee, which ended a career that included four Pro Bowls, one of which he'd decided with a blocked extra point. His greatest game was the four-interception game on December 13, 1953 in Washington. Eddie LeBaron was the opposing quarterback.

"Bill Dudley was with the 'Skins then and he ran a down and out," Butler said. "He was at the end of his career; I was on the right corner. But it was a down and out, and LeBaron threw it to him and I came up and it was an easy pick and I went straight down the field. I just don't remember much more about it. I remember that play, but I just never thought four interceptions was that great of a thing."

Butler returned the interception for the deciding touchdown in the Steelers' 14-13 win. A month earlier, Butler, playing wide receiver, beat Frank Gifford for the winning touchdown against the New York Giants. In his career, Butler scored four offensive touchdowns and five defensive touchdowns. Finks once complained that his passing statistics suffered because Butler was used so much on defense.

As well as Butler could catch, he was better known for his hitting. He could not only strike the blow, Butler wrapped up. But what does John Bradshaw Butler remember most about playing defense in the 1950s?

"Jim Brown was hard to bring down," he said. "If you hit him hard, you took as much punishment. Ollie Matson had lot of speed. [Hugh] McElhenny was a great back; so were [Marion] Motley, Eddie Price.

"I remember it was a great life, really great. The '50s were good years. I just loved the game and loved to play. Everything was a challenge. I mean I loved it. Playing the Browns, it was great—Mac Speedie or Dante Lavelli, playing whomever, covering so and so. He wasn't going to beat me; I was going to beat him. I thought that way anyway. Those were just great years."

CHAPTER 5

Pat
Brady

Art Rooney Sr. liked to tell the story of how the Steelers signed Pat Brady, whom the Chief considered the best punter "in the National League, or anywhere else, for that matter." According to a news-service story, Brady sent the first punt of a 1952 tryout into the far bleachers of the Steelers' training facility at St. Bonaventure University. Rooney said the ball traveled 120 yards.

"Make it 150," Brady said from his ranch almost 54 years later.

Brady fits the stereotype of the wise-cracking punter, but contacting him wasn't easy. If the 78-year-old wasn't fishing Alaska's Kenai River for King Salmon, he was locating used cars for his business partner or irrigating his 70-acre homestead in Reno, Nevada. Today, a day in which the temperature would soar to 103 degrees, Brady took the late-morning call just before cracking open a Corona.

"Every time I turn around I've got more horseshit to take care of," he said as he settled into his easy chair.

The Steelers signed Brady in 1952 and he performed so well in only three years that he was named to their all-time team in 1982. A left-footed kicker, Brady holds the NCAA record for the longest punt. In 1950 he boomed one 99 yards for Nevada-Reno. The school later dropped the sport, so Brady, who also played quarterback, transferred to Bradley University. He was drafted by the New York Giants in 1952, but went to the Canadian Football League instead. The Hamilton Tiger-Cats released him, though, because the few Americans allowed on each roster were asked to do more than just kick. So Steelers equipment manager Jack Lee convinced Rooney to bring Brady in for a look.

"His claim to fame is he discovered me," Brady said of Lee. "So I went down there, punted a couple. The whole team was there—Mr. Rooney was there—so I stayed."

In his first year with the Steelers, Brady averaged 43.2 yards per punt. The next year, 1953, he led the NFL in punts (80), yards (3,752) and average (46.9). He again led the NFL in 1954 with an average punt of 43.2 yards. Brady's short career came to an end during a 1955 preseason game against the Philadelphia Eagles. Brady jumped for a high snap from rookie center Fred Broussard, came down and snapped his left Achilles tendon.

"When I came down I could feel a bang," Brady said. "Before I even punted I turned around and thought the referee had kicked me in the leg. Then I went ahead and walked on it, which you're not supposed to be able to do, then punted the ball and it went 30 yards."

Dr. Phil Faix, a physician for the local hockey team, was an expert on the injury, but he couldn't save Brady's career.

"It shortened my step just a bit," Brady said. "He told me I'd stretched it out over a period of time, and if I did snapped it again he'd have to cut something out and I'd have a gimp, so I said forget it."

Brady retired with a career average of 44.5, second in team history to Bobby Joe Green's 45.7. Records from the period are sketchy, but Brady said his longest pro punt went 89 yards. "But they only gave me credit for 78 because I was standing in my end zone," he said. "It was in Green Bay, about a minute to go, we were winning by a point and the guy caught it. If that had gotten over him it would've went into the end zone. If that guy hadn't caught that at about the 12-yard line, I'd hold both records. It'd be nice to hold both of them."

How did Brady punt a 99-yarder in college anyway? "They used to call the winds around here Konapah Lo," he said. "It's a helluva whirlwind that used to come through this valley. That's what they all said, that it was the Konapah Lo, but it just got over the safety man's head and rolled."

Brady was born in Seattle and went off to play quarterback at the University of Oregon, but coach Jim Aiken (1947-50, .512) told Brady he wouldn't play there ahead of Norm Van Brocklin. So as the Ducks headed for a berth in the Sugar Bowl, Brady headed for Reno, a place he'd eventually call home.

Brady and his wife, Odile, went back to Reno after his playing days ended. The two have remained together—53 years and counting—and raised five kids. After football, Brady entered the printing business. He received a break when Nevada Governor Mike O'Callaghan named him superintendent of state printing in 1971. Brady's office handled all of the printing for the state, from files to business cards.

When O'Callaghan ("the greatest governor we ever had," said Brady) left office in 1979, so did Brady. He had purchased the Bonanza Casino a few years

PAT BRADY
Seasons with Steelers: 1952-54
Position: punter
Height: 6-foot-1
Playing weight: 195 pounds

earlier and bought his ranch soon thereafter, so he had plenty on his plate. The Bonanza is a 14,000-square-foot casino located about three miles north of downtown Reno. Brady owned it for nearly 25 years before selling.

"It's just a neighborhood place where we had a little fun and tried to make some money from time to time," said Brady. "I enjoyed it for a long period. Once you find a place where you're kind of halfway happy, then you stay there and that's what I did."

Is Brady much of a gambler?

"Nope," he said. "Once you own a place you never gamble. You see how big the hotels are? Somebody must have paid for that."

Brady sold the Bonanza, but "it's still in operation. I sold out about three and a half years ago," he said. "I just wanted to get out and do something else. I wanted a little time to work on the ranch, which I couldn't do in the morning with the casino. I had to do my work in the afternoon."

And that's not feasible in the Reno sun, no matter how many ranch hands Brady had available.

"I ran everybody off," he said. "The main thing is the water. You've got to play with the water and follow the water to get it just where you want it."

What's up with the water?

"Hay," he said. "Hay for the cows; hay for anybody. Hell, if I get hungry enough, I'll eat it."

"Actually, I shouldn't even have the damn thing," he said of the ranch. "There are so goddamn many houses going up around here it should go on the market. And I'm tired of irrigating, but everybody's been after it. It's the last piece probably in the valley and everybody wants it, so I don't know."

Would it bring big money? "I don't know about that. The government's right behind you. I don't know. I might keep a little piece for us—the house and two or three acres, a couple of horses. It's somewhere I can go."

It serves as a rest stop between his adventures. In the summer of 2005, he took his son to southern Alaska.

"He just got back from the war zone and I promised to take him someplace where he could relax and catch some fish."

Brady also has a day job: He locates cars. For a fee, he said, customers can save close to $8,000 on a year-old car with 20,000 miles on it in perfect condition.

"I have a partner that does most of the work," Brady said. "I just sit around and drink beer."

And sometimes he'll reminisce about his days with the Steelers.

"One of the greatest guys I remember there was Jim Finks," Brady said of the Steelers' first T-formation quarterback.

"He was heady, a heady guy, but he didn't have the equipment; by that I mean the guys outside to do the job for him. He made up everything on the field by himself. A lot of quarterbacks did at the time, but Jim was a little sharper than most of them. He just pulled out stunts nobody else expected.

"It was just a bunch of good guys. We didn't have a prima donna. I saw all those guys, about 20 of them, at a reunion a couple years ago. If you call one of them and they say something about me, call me back and I'll tell you it was a lie."

Brady and the Steelers were 11-13 in 1952-53 under Joe Bach. In 1954, under Walt Kiesling, the Steelers were 5-7. In 1955, Kiesling—in spite of an urgent letter from 15-year-old Timmy Rooney to the racetrack-visiting Chief—cut rookie quarterback John Unitas.

"Unitas was my roommate," Brady said. "That's my only claim to fame, that they cut Unitas and kept me. It's my only claim to fame."

But soon thereafter, Brady went down with the injury.

"I'd liked to have been around awhile," he said. "I'd have been on some kind of all-time deal like Ray Guy. He was around for 14 years [42.4 average]. He was no better than me. Maybe if I'd have been there several years I could've earned that kind of reputation. But you can't look back. You've got to keep moving."

CHAPTER 6

Ted Marchibroda

Another in the long line of NFL quarterbacks from Western Pennsylvania, Ted Marchibroda went on to enjoy greater success in the NFL as a coach. In fact, his list of pupils represents a who's who of star offensive players. Marchibroda coached Roman Gabriel, Larry Brown, Bert Jones, and Jim Harbaugh through MVP seasons, and he turned Billy Kilmer into one of the NFL's great comeback stories of the early 1970s. Jim Kelly thanked Marchibroda in the first paragraph of his Hall of Fame acceptance speech. From taking play calls from the president of the United States to watching his receiver drop what would've been the most significant Hail Mary pass of all time, Marchibroda has run the coaching gamut, and it all started way back in Franklin, Pennsylvania, a small town situated some 85 miles north of Pittsburgh. That's where Marchibroda was born and raised, and where he learned to play the game.

"Small-town living is good," said Marchibroda. "The people are good; they're very considerate. I think it helped me from a standpoint, as I look back, that I lived on one side of town and you played the guys on the other side of town that you thought were different. You weren't quite sure of what you were running into. The reason I say this is in football—coaching football—you're dealing with people. The Xs and Os I believe are secondary. It sort of helped me get along with people."

Marchibroda was born in 1931 and went to college at St. Bonaventure, where the Steelers trained. There he played for Joe Bach and learned the T-formation. Marchibroda broke Eastern Intercollegiate Football records before the school dropped football in 1952. He transferred to the University of Detroit and led the nation in total offense in 1952. His 390 passing yards against Tulsa was a national record at the time.

In 1953, with Bach as their coach, the Steelers chose Marchibroda with the fifth pick of the draft. The 5-foot-10, 178-pounder saw spot duty behind Jim

PITTSBURGH STEELERS IMAGE LIBRARY

TED MARCHIBRODA
Seasons with Steelers: 1953, 1955-56
Position: quarterback
Height: 5-foot-10
Playing weight: 178 pounds

Finks before being called into the army. Marchibroda returned in 1955 and took over the starting job in 1956. He completed 45 percent of his passes with 12 touchdowns and 19 interceptions as the Steelers went 5-7 under Walt Kiesling.

"Jimmy retired and I started," Marchibroda recalled. "I always remember winning the opening ball game. We played the Redskins in Pittsburgh. [Eddie] LeBaron was the starting quarterback for the Redskins and I started for the Steelers. To give you an indication of how things have changed, how big they are now, it was almost like two midgets starting. But we won the opener, I remember that, and that it was a good ballgame."

With his scrambling style, Marchibroda led the Steelers to a 30-13 win over the Redskins and their 5-9 quarterback. The Steelers then lost three in a row before posting one of their biggest wins of the decade.

"I was the first [Steelers] quarterback to beat the Browns in Cleveland," Marchibroda said. "It was a thrill because the Browns were so dominant in those years."

The Steelers beat the Browns, 24-16, in 1956. It was only the second time the Steelers had defeated them in 14 tries. It occurred the year after Otto Graham retired; the year before Jim Brown was drafted.

The addition of 1957 first-round pick Len Dawson and new coach Buddy Parker—who traded two No. 1 draft picks to San Francisco for Earl Morrall—meant the end for Marchibroda. He was released before the 1957 season and was picked up by the Chicago Cardinals. He played one more season before an arm injury forced him to retire.

There were other significant moments for Marchibroda during his time in Pittsburgh. He married his wife, Ann, in 1954. The two raised four children and recently celebrated their 50th anniversary at home in Weems, Virginia. In 1956, Marchibroda became one of the first quarterbacks to wear a radio receiver in his helmet. Paul Brown used the device earlier that season, but Marchibroda and Kiesling didn't have the same luck with their "electronic quarterback." On October 14, in a loss to the Philadelphia Eagles at Forbes Field, Marchibroda heard nothing but static from Kiesling. The device was outlawed later that year by Commissioner Bert Bell.

With the Steelers, Marchibroda impressed lineman Bill McPeak, and when McPeak became coach of the Washington Redskins in 1961 he made Marchibroda part of his staff. Marchibroda stayed there five years before becoming George Allen's offensive coordinator with the Los Angeles Rams in 1966. With the Rams, Marchibroda developed Gabriel into the 1969 MVP before returning to the Redskins with Allen in 1971.

"With McPeak, all the coaches were former ball players. We had Bucko Kilroy, Ernie Stautner, George Wilson, Abe Gibron, so there I learned the Xs and Os," Marchibroda said. "With George Allen, I learned organization and hard work. I would say George was really my mentor. I spent nine years with him."

And they never had a losing season. The Redskins made the playoffs in 1971, but were eliminated by the San Francisco 49ers in a game noted for a disastrous play called by President Richard Nixon. Nixon, the legend goes, called Allen earlier in the week to suggest a flanker reverse by Roy Jefferson. Marchibroda signaled the play to Kilmer after the Redskins reached the 49ers' 8-yard line in the second quarter. Jefferson lost 13 yards on the play and a subsequent field-goal attempt was blocked. The Redskins lost by four points.

Marchibroda takes the blame for the play call. "He really had nothing to do with us running it," he said of Nixon. "It was my play call. We thought we had a touchdown, but Cedrick Hardman, the defensive end, made an outstanding play. He bit on play-action to begin with, but made a tremendous recovery and threw us for a loss. It was going to be a big play for us."

In 1972, Kilmer and MVP Brown led the Redskins to the Super Bowl, where they lost to the undefeated Miami Dolphins, 14-7. Two weeks after the game, the Baltimore Colts drafted Bert Jones with the second pick of the draft. He struggled for two years before the Colts hired Marchibroda as head coach in 1975.

"They felt he needed a quarterback coach," Marchibroda explained.

The Colts got that and more. Not only did Jones enjoy his three best pro seasons (MVP in 1976) under Marchibroda, the coach turned the Colts into instant contenders. Their 10-4 record in 1975 was the greatest one-year turnaround in NFL history (prior to 16-game schedules). It netted Marchibroda several coach-of-the-year awards and his team a berth in the playoffs, where the Colts were eliminated by the Steelers, 28-10.

Marchibroda also gave a 22-year-old by the name of Bill Belichick his coaching start in 1975. Originally hired for two season tickets and room and board at training camp, Belichick so impressed Marchibroda that he had management pay Belichick $25 a week. The next year, when Marchibroda asked management to give Belichick a salary of $4,000, Belichick was fired.

"I couldn't say that I saw greatness, but he was very hard working," Marchibroda said. "If you gave him an assignment, you didn't see him again until the assignment was completed. You never had to correct him. He'd lock himself in that room, and you wouldn't see him until he was through."

The 1976 season was an odd one for Marchibroda. It began with an in-house conflict that led to his resignation, but he was called back after the players threatened to revolt. The season ended with a private plane crashing into Memorial Stadium following a 40-14 playoff loss to the Steelers.

"The guy drove over to our practice on Thursday prior to the ball game and he dropped a tie onto the field," Marchibroda said. "I don't think there was any significance to it. We didn't know it was the same guy until after he crashed. I think the significance was people talked about the crash more than they talked about our defeat."

Marchibroda was fired in 1979 after back-to-back 5-11 seasons. He returned to prominence in 1987 as the Buffalo Bills' offensive coordinator. With the help of Kelly, Marchibroda developed the breakneck "K-Gun" offense and was with the Bills in their first two Super Bowl appearances.

"Over the years you use the same system and you try to improve upon it and it all came together in Buffalo," Marchibroda said. "Jim wanted to call the plays. That was a big plus for us. Jim loved to be the head. He loved it. He really did, so that was all part of the success."

Marchibroda returned to the Colts in 1992 and led them to the 1995 AFC Championship game at Pittsburgh. As 12-point underdogs, the Colts came within a dropped Hail Mary pass from Harbaugh of defeating the Steelers and advancing to the Super Bowl.

"There were two things about that ball game," Marchibroda said. "You didn't see Kordell [Stewart] step out of bounds did you? That was the first part. I don't think you expect a fellow to step out of bounds in the end zone and come back in to catch a touchdown. I can't ever remember that happening in 36 years of coaching. As far as the last play, the Hail Mary play, I could see the players raising their hands as though it were a touchdown, but I was focused on the official because that's the final decision. In that period, in between them raising their hands and the official saying 'incomplete,' I felt we won the ball game."

As a head coach, Marchibroda was 2-4 in the playoffs. Three of the four losses were administered by the Steelers.

"Well, I could understand why we lost the first two," he recalled. "I mean, they were a good football team. They were as fine of a football team that's ever been in the National Football League. But the third one hurt a little bit."

Insulted by a one-year contract offer after the 1995 season, Marchibroda resigned. He was hired by the Baltimore Ravens—the year they left Cleveland—but won only 16 games from 1996 through 1998 and was fired.

"If I had to do it all over again, I don't think I'd take a job with a team that's been transferred from one city to another. There are just too many problems that you wouldn't ordinarily have," he said.

Marchibroda became a radio color analyst for Colts games in 2001. He entered his fifth season on the job in 2005.

"I enjoy it because the Colts are my team," he said before the season began. "They're the team to watch right now."

Of course, they *were* the team to watch. The Colts were the top seed in the AFC—the conference that was favored to win the Super Bowl by 10 points at the onset of the playoffs—but were upset in first round of the playoffs by, yes, the Pittsburgh Steelers.

CHAPTER 7

John Lattner

The Steelers have drafted two Heisman Trophy winners and signed one. While Doc Blanchard of Army opted to serve his country, John Lattner of Notre Dame signed with the Steelers, but played only one season, 1954, before an injury ended his career. Lattner may be forgotten in Pittsburgh, but he's still so big in his hometown of Chicago that he leads the mighty St. Patrick's Day parade every year.

"I've had those same kilts on me since 1966," Lattner said. "I look like I've gone through the wars."

Born on the West Side of Chicago, Lattner starred at Fenwick High before attending Notre Dame, where he won the 1953 Heisman. He also set the school record for most fumbles in a game, a feat that's provided Lattner with after-dinner speech fodder ever since.

"The only reason I stayed in the game long enough to fumble five times," he said, "is that Leahy kept me in for defense. But that's my only record as a football player at Notre Dame."

That was 1952, and he did win the Maxwell Award as the nation's best college football player that year. In 1953, Lattner led Notre Dame to a 9-0-1 record in Frank Leahy's final season as coach. Lattner repeated as the Maxwell winner and also won the Heisman, giving him iconic status in his hometown. Lattner is still the only Notre Dame running back to have won a Heisman. After playing in 421 of a possible 600 minutes as a two-way All-American his senior year, Lattner was drafted by the Steelers with the seventh pick of the 1954 draft.

As a rookie, the 195-pound halfback gained 237 yards rushing, caught 25 passes for 305 yards, returned punts and kickoffs, and scored seven touchdowns. He made the Pro Bowl as a rookie, but never played for the Steelers again.

JOHN LATTNER
Seasons with Steelers: 1954
Position: running back
Height: 6-foot-1
Playing weight: 195 pounds

"I was ROTC at Notre Dame, Air Force ROTC, so before we went into service they let us play one year of pro football, and so I played in '54 and went into the service in March of '55," he said.

Lattner was stationed in Washington, D.C. at Bolling Air Force Base. He tore an ACL playing football in 1955 and spent 1956 rehabbing. Lattner made a comeback with the Steelers in 1957, but his knee couldn't take it. At Buffalo, in the final exhibition game, he decided he was done.

"I didn't have a lot of speed anyway, so I figured with the bad knee and the swelling I'd better retire. I told Mr. Rooney after the game I was going to retire. He said, 'Well, we don't want you to retire, John. Are you sure?' I said I was."

Lattner went back to Chicago to work for a petroleum company before taking a job coaching high-school football in Kenosha, Wisconsin. St. Joseph went 5-2-1 in 1958, and Lattner moved on to the University of Denver as a backfield coach for two years.

"We weren't that successful," he said. "They didn't fire us, but they gave up football, so I gave up coaching."

So he went back to Chicago and opened Johnny Lattner's Steak House at the corner of Madison and Clark. The restaurant lasted five and a half years before a fire destroyed the building and his Heisman Trophy. When he opened Johnny Lattner's Marina City Restaurant, Lattner sent pictures of the burned and broken trophy to the Downtown Athletic Club and he was sent a replacement for $300.

"I put it on the piano bar," Lattner said. "Somebody said, 'Well, isn't that kind of dangerous John? Don't you think somebody will steal it?' I said by the time they got to the front door, they'd have a hernia [from trying to carry it]. I never really was too concerned about it."

Lattner also had trouble holding onto his Heisman ring. It was stolen out of his gym locker in 2000. The Oak Park police sent a description of the ring to every pawn shop on the North Side of Chicago. The owner of one of the pawn shops had been warned about dealing in stolen goods only a few weeks earlier by police, so he called the police as soon as the ring thief walked in with his latest haul.

"The guy called the police station because he thought he was being set up," Lattner said. "And the two Irish cops came over and they chased the guy with the bags into the Dunkin' Donuts about a block from the police station. The only customers who go there are the policemen from the station, so they caught him, called me up, and I got the ring back."

After five and a half years running the Marina City Restaurant, Lattner grew weary of the business and went back to selling printing with his brother-in-law.

"Right after lunch on Mondays we used to report to the Law Auditorium," Lattner said. "Leahy would go through the previous game, the mistakes we made. His first few comments from the stage—and I was in the first row—were: 'Oh my God lads, last Saturday against the enemy there's a lad who disgraced his mommy and daddy and his coaching staff here at the University of Notre Dame and disgraced his teammates and our Lady of the Dome by his five fumbles.' He didn't mention my name; that's how he was."

After the team meeting, Leahy met with Lattner. Leahy asked if he was having girl trouble, to which Lattner said no. Then Leahy asked if he liked to bet the horses, to which Lattner said yes.

"Then he said, 'I was just wondering, John, did you have any money bet with the West Side bookies last Saturday against Purdue?'

"He thought I was betting on the game. I said no, Coach, I don't have any money now and I didn't have any money on the game. It really threw me for a loss, but he wanted to get to the crux of why I fumbled. Then he said to me, 'I'd like to have you do one little favor. After this little meeting, I'd like you to go to one of the chapels here at the University of Notre Dame, and John, I'd like to have you go to confession and confess those five mortal sins.'

"It's hard to believe, but it's the truth. Naturally I didn't go there. He did give me a football, and I had to carry it around wherever I went on campus. He said that if he caught me without it, he'd take my scholarship away. I did carry it around and one of my teammates put a handle on it. The only positive that came out of that was I think the professors felt sorry for me and I got good grades that semester."

"We're in the computer forms business and we broker all kinds of print
he said. "Anything that's printable, we can print."

What does Lattner remember about his year with the Steelers? "Scarec
said with a laugh.

Lattner recalled a hamstring injury that dogged his training camp
Bonaventure. He opened the season at Green Bay as the second-team ha
behind Lynn Chandnois and scored a touchdown in the opener. The S
beat the Packers and then the Redskins.

"We're 2-0; we're leading the Eastern Division," he said. "Fans are s
to come out to witness what the heck this was all about. The third game
season we played the (2-0) Eagles at Connie Mack Stadium and we lost t
by two points. I can remember the play: It was fourth down and about a
go and they gave me the ball, and I swear to God I made the foot. I s
God."

The Steelers led the Eagles 22-17 at the time, but Lattner was rule
and the Steelers turned the ball over on downs at the 18. The Eagles c
yards for the game-winning touchdown.

"Then we played the Cleveland Browns at Forbes Field, a
afternoon," he recalled. "They had Otto Graham. They had a pretty gc
that year. We beat them, 55-27. It was unbelievable. Ray Mathews
bunch of touchdown passes; Jimmy Finks had a beautiful day; our de
playing real well. So we were 3-1. Then we played the Eagles again on a
night. Elbie Nickel catches a touchdown pass and we win and we're le
league at 4-1. Then we went to Chicago, Comiskey Park, to play the C
who hadn't won a game. We had a couple of key defensive linemen out,
Matson ran a kickoff back 91 yards to beat us 17-14. That was our de
didn't win another game until we played the Cardinals back at Forbe
we ended up 5-7.

"I was kind of satisfied with myself. I made some rookie mistakes
invited to the Pro Bowl game. It wasn't televised in those days; they bi
on the radio, but they played the game at the Coliseum in Los Ang
the Heisman award winner, I think, helped me make the Pro Bowl. T
advertisements, but others were more deserving.

"I look back and can say I played one year in pro football and I
that bad. Those are big boys. They knock you around. It's a tough li
know what? The money wasn't really that great. Most guys had two jc
came fast and I figured I'd better go to work."

Lattner remains a sought-after banquet speaker. His fa
continues to be the five-fumble game at Purdue and Leahy's reactic

CHAPTER 8

John Reger

United Press International reported nothing out of the ordinary in its lead paragraph about the Steelers' 1955 opener against the Chicago Cardinals: "Pittsburgh sports fans never hesitate to boo their own heroes, but they're probably feeling a little sheepish today over their latest attack on quarterback Jim Finks."

No, nothing unusual there. But there was something unusual about the paper's dateline the day after the game was played. It read: Tuesday, September 27. Yes, the Steelers played a Monday night football game at Forbes Field to open the 1955 season. The Pirates held the venue through the weekend and the Steelers were forced to wait, but a hefty crowd of 26,359 showed up and surprised the UPI correspondent. So did the play of rookie linebacker John Reger.

Finks was the primary focus. His fourth-quarter interception was returned 92 yards for a Cardinals touchdown that tied the game 7-7. He redeemed himself with a last-minute touchdown pass to Ray Mathews for a late 14-7 lead. The Cardinals had one more chance in the final seconds, and quarterback Lamar McHan dropped back and looked for Hall of Famer Ollie Matson, but Reger dropped in coverage and intercepted the pass to end the game.

The rookie wanted to keep the souvenir from his debut, but after the referee cleared the celebrating Steelers off the field, he ordered one more play for the Steelers' offense.

"That cost me a football," Reger said. "The ref threw me off when he ordered another play, so Elbie Nickel finally got it."

And Nickel gave the ball to Mathews. Reger didn't mind. He thought he'd already received the biggest break a player could get: He'd made the team without playing college football, or much of it anyway.

Reger had been a significant Pitt recruit out of The Linsly School in Wheeling, West Virginia. Reger grew up in Wheeling with a brother and five sisters. He was given a scholarship to the private military school and then chose Pitt from a number of offers from around the country. At Pitt, Reger helped the freshman team to an undefeated season, but after only two varsity games his sophomore season Reger injured his knee and Pitt took away his scholarship.

Married to wife Janice, who took care of their five-year-old daughter, Kathy, Reger was forced to work two jobs after his $90 payments were pulled. Four years later, with the help of high school coach Etx Rine and a recommendation from John Michelosen that compared Reger to Joe Schmidt, Reger was granted a tryout by the Steelers. The tryout turned into a starting job after the Steelers lost to the San Francisco 49ers, 60-14, in a 1955 exhibition game in Sacramento. Reger was named the right outside linebacker by an upset coach Walt Kiesling, and Reger didn't lose the job until he was cut, along with five others, in a similar post-exhibition game snit thrown by Buddy Parker nine years later.

In those nine years, Reger was a fixture for the rugged Steelers defense. He was named to Pro Bowls following the 1959, 1960, and 1961 seasons. Jack Butler called Reger "the best linebacker in the league" in 1958, when the Steelers finished as the league's top-ranked defense. At the time, the consensus was that New York's Sam Huff was the best linebacker in the game. Reger called Huff overrated at the time, and stands by the statement, even though it was considered heresy at the time.

"I think he was overrated," Reger said from his home in Tampa. "He was always piling on, and then they'd say, 'Tackle by Sam Huff' over the loudspeaker, when all he did was jump on the pile. He was a good player but they really blew it out of proportion. Now, Chuck Bednarik, who was a helluva nice guy, he was good. He played. He tackled. But Sam Huff, I remember him when we went to Pro Bowls. He was in the middle and I played the right side and Bednarik played the left side, and it was the same thing. You'd always hear his name mentioned at The Coliseum in Los Angeles, and it'd be the same thing: He'd pile on and get the credit for everything. Not that it bothered me. I just answered someone's question at the time."

Reger was the Steelers' defensive captain and player rep through the late 1950s and early 1960s. He was a 6-foot, 225-pounder with a nose for the football. In a career that stretched 12 years, Reger intercepted 15 passes and returned three turnovers for touchdowns.

"We had a good defense. The game was fun to play," Reger said. "It was football in those days, do you know what I mean? Today's football, to me, it

PITTSBURGH STEELERS IMAGE LIBRARY

JOHN REGER
Seasons with Steelers: 1955-63
Position: outside linebacker
Height: 6 feet
Playing weight: 225 pounds

seems all they're trying to do is hurt somebody. They knock the quarterback down and stand there and point every which way. We used to love to knock the quarterback down, but then we'd reach our hand down and help him back up. Let him play another one; maybe he'd throw you an interception or something."

In his playing days, Reger owned a service station on Ohio River Boulevard in Belleview and a restaurant called The Sports Bar in McKees Rocks. Both businesses were financed by Art Rooney.

"Every ballplayer had to show up at my bar after the game was over," Reger said. "You had to show up and you could bring your wife or your girlfriend and it cost you five dollars apiece and you had all you could eat, all you could drink, and live music. Buddy Parker always wanted everybody to get together, win or lose, after the game. He always said, 'Everybody shows up.' And then he'd say, 'If you don't like it, leave, but show up.' I got along real good with him."

Reger has kind words for his former coach, but Parker embarrassed Reger and five others after a 42-7 exhibition loss to the Browns in 1964. The Steelers had flown to Akron from their training camp in Kingston, Rhode Island, for the mauling, and Reger and running back Preston Carpenter didn't fly back. Four other players were cut upon the team's return to the University of Rhode Island campus, where the Steelers trained before the 1964 and 1965 seasons.

"He said, 'I'm getting rid of all you old farts,'" Reger said. "That's exactly what he said when he let me go. But I was in good shape; no problem. I went to the Redskins, and every game I played against Pittsburgh I won."

Reger finished his career with the Washington Redskins. His former teammate with the Steelers, Bill McPeak, was the Redskins' coach and he felt Reger had something left. He even upped Reger's salary from $18,000 with the Steelers to $25,000. Reger played three years in Washington.

"I think my problem with Buddy started the year before," Reger said. "I was hurt. In fact, I almost got killed."

In the Steelers' 1963 season opener at Franklin Field in Philadelphia, Reger went low to tackle running back Theron Sapp, and Reger's head met Sapp's knee. Reger was knocked out cold and taken from the field on a stretcher. He missed five games with a concussion.

"I was dead on the field," Reger said. "At first I could hear people hollering, 'Get a doctor! Get an ambulance! He's falling out!' Then I woke up in a hospital in Philadelphia, and about an hour later they flew my wife in."

According to newspaper accounts of the game, Reger "swallowed his tongue."

"They thought I did," he said. "And they broke a lot of my teeth prying open my mouth, but I just needed oxygen, and when the ambulance came out on the field they put the oxygen on me and that snapped it right away and I started breathing and was alright. But from that day on, there's been oxygen on the sidelines. They didn't have any oxygen on the sideline. If there wasn't any in the ambulance I probably would've been dead."

After Reger was cut by the Steelers, his spot at right linebacker was taken by Andy Russell, whose 18 interceptions in 12 seasons topped Reger's total. After his career ended, Reger formed a landscaping business in Hollywood, Florida. Then he bought a restaurant in Tampa, which he owned for 15 years.

"The league used to have conventions in Hollywood, Florida," he said. "That's how I ended up down here. In '59 they all voted me to represent them, the player rep. It took a little guts to do it but it worked out great. We got pensions. Most everything we have today came through in 1959 and that was the pension. It made me feel pretty good."

Janice, Reger's wife of 46 years, died in 1996. His daughter, Kathy, is a nurse in Orlando and his son, John Jr., is a PGA golf pro in Gainesville. He visits his dad once a week when he drives to Tampa to do a radio show. Reger said he's still a fan of the Steelers.

"Everybody down here is. There are Pittsburgh fans everywhere," he said. "All these little bars, they have the Steeler game on. I watched the Super Bowl at the bar and signed autographs and stuff.

"I enjoyed my time with the Steelers. I had a great time. I still get bubblegum cards from people to sign and people wanting pictures and everything else. I do it. I go up to the store and have them make me about 10 or 20 of them and send them back. If they're thinking about me, I might as well keep them in mind too."

CHAPTER 9

Len
Dawson

Paul Brown knew nothing but success in his first six seasons in the NFL. He brought the Cleveland Browns into the NFL in 1950 and the team went 58-13-1 with a 3-3 record in NFL Championship games. But quarterback Otto Graham retired before the 1956 season, and the Browns crashed to 5-7. This was not acceptable to Brown, who wanted a young quarterback. Brown liked two college quarterbacks in particular: Stanford's John Brodie and Purdue's Len Dawson.

Dawson was a three-time Big Ten passing and total offense leader at Purdue, and best of all he was a local kid. Dawson grew up a Browns fan in Alliance, Ohio, so Brown put his connections to work. Dawson's college coach was Jack Mollenkipf and he'd coached high-school ball at Toledo-Waite while Brown coached at Massillon. Brown figured Brodie would be gone and that the Pittsburgh Steelers—who were to flip a coin with the Browns for the fifth pick of the 1957 draft—would draft Dawson. So Brown asked his old friend Mollenkipf for a favor. Since the Canadian Football League held its draft before the NFL, would Mollenkipf ask Dawson to announce before the coin toss that he was going to play in the CFL?

"He figured if Pittsburgh won and read that, they wouldn't pick me," Dawson said almost 50 years later. "All coaches are looking for an edge, but I said, hell no. I'm not even going to pretend I'm going that route. So Pittsburgh won the toss and selected me, and poor old Paul Brown had to settle for the guy from Syracuse."

Of course, the guy from Syracuse was running back Jim Brown. Walt Kiesling and the Steelers drafted Dawson, but Kiesling resigned soon thereafter because of health problems. Buddy Parker, who'd quit as the coach of the Detroit Lions, became coach of the Steelers, and that was the first strike against Dawson.

"Buddy was a strange dude," Dawson said. "We were playing Philadelphia late in the season and I hadn't played at all. It was getting cold, and I was putting on long johns and all that stuff to keep warm during the game. As we were walking into the locker room he said, 'Get ready, you're starting.' I thought, dear God, what is with this guy? I hadn't played all season and barely practiced that week, but I went in and took off some of my clothes so I could maneuver around a little bit. I only played the first half and he took me out."

The Steelers lost 7-6. Dawson completed two-of-four passes but was yanked after his second-quarter fumble set up the Eagles' only touchdown.

Dawson's Steelers highlights came in games that didn't count. In his first exhibition game, against the Chicago Bears, Dawson's first pass went for a touchdown to Ralph Jelic. It left Art Rooney enthused. "That Dawson boy is going to be a good one," the Chief told reporters. Between that game and the season opener, Parker became the coach. His first move was to trade two first-round draft picks to San Francisco for Earl Morrall. And when Parker acquired his former back-up in Detroit, Jack Kemp, he released Ted Marchibroda and Jack Scarbath.

"Everybody was on eggshells," Dawson recalled. "The veterans told me, 'Keep your bags packed and your belly full because those buses leave all the time and you might be on the next one.' That was the case, particularly with Buddy. And Buddy Parker never played rookies at any position."

Quarterbacks Morrall, Dawson, and Kemp would combine for 50 years of pro service, 40.2 miles of passing yardage, 16 Pro Bowls, nine championships, three MVP trophies, a spot in the Hall of Fame, and seats in the Cabinet and the U.S. House of Representatives, but the Steelers struggled with them. They went 6-6 in 1957, and the break-up of the young triumvirate began in the 1958 training camp when Parker cut Kemp for disobeying an order to punt the ball out of bounds during an exhibition game. The punt was returned for a touchdown and Kemp was off to the CFL.

Morrall was the next to go. After a humiliating defeat at home to the Browns early in 1958, the Steelers were 0-2. Morrall had thrown one touchdown pass against seven interceptions in those games.

"The loss to Cleveland killed Buddy," Dawson said. "After the game he said, 'Generally I tell you to go out and get drunk to solve your problems, but this time I want you to go home and figure out what's wrong because tomorrow we're going to find out what's wrong and we're going to fix it.'"

Parker's idea of fixing a problem was to make a trade, so he sent Morrall—along with a second-round pick that year and a fourth-round pick in 1960

LEN DAWSON
Seasons with Steelers: 1957-59
Position: quarterback
Height: 6 feet
Playing weight: 190 pounds

(Roger Brown)—to the Detroit Lions for Bobby Layne. Dawson sat the bench behind Layne all of 1958 and 1959. In three seasons with the Steelers, the 1957 first-round draft pick attempted 17 passes and completed six with one touchdown.

Dawson's best appearance with the Steelers came during a 1959 exhibition game against the Chicago Cardinals in Austin, Texas, where Layne had attended the University of Texas. In his first appearance since leaving college 12 years earlier, Layne played the first half before Dawson entered to complete five of seven passes for 120 yards in the second half. The Steelers lost the game, but that didn't stop Layne from partying. He was arrested later that night for drunken driving after wrecking into a parked car and fleeing the scene in a taxicab.

Layne spent five hours in jail the same night he'd been serenaded with "The Eyes of Texas Are Upon You." He took a plaque and his starting job back to Pittsburgh, but left $300 and his license in Austin.

"He was unique, I'll say that," Dawson said. "That guy was cut out of a different mold somewhere along the line. He used to always say, 'I'm going to run out of money and breath at the same time,' and I think he tried."

After the 1959 season, Dawson was traded to the Browns, along with Gern Nagler, for Junior Wren and Preston Carpenter. But Dawson didn't play much in Cleveland, either. He cracked ribs in an automobile accident two weeks before rookie camp and wasn't able to throw. He sat behind Milt Plum in 1960.

In 1961, Dawson started his second NFL game, and it was against the Steelers. Plum was out with a dislocated thumb, and Dawson—unlike his previous start—had a week to prepare. But in his enthusiasm, Dawson threw so much that his arm was sore by game day. He didn't tell Brown, and he struggled. Dawson completed six of 12 passes for 68 yards, and the Browns trailed by 14-10 when Plum replaced him late in the second quarter. The Browns rallied to win at Forbes Field, 30-28.

Dawson considered quitting but contemplated an old offer from his former backfield coach at Purdue, Hank Stram. The two had lunch during a convention in Pittsburgh in 1960. The American Football League was born that year, and Dawson told Stram of his struggles. Stram said that Dawson couldn't play for him unless he was released by the Browns. So after the 1961 season Dawson approached Brown and asked to be traded. A week later, Brown called Dawson into his office and told him there was no interest, so Dawson asked for and was given his release. The rest became AFL history.

Dawson sold his home in Allison Park, joined Stram with the Dallas Texans, and, after a summer of knocking off the rust, led the Texans to the AFL title and was named the AFL Most Valuable Player in 1962. After five years of inactivity, Dawson blossomed in his sixth. The old rule of thumb held that quarterbacks didn't realize their potential until five years or so. Was this the case?

"I heard that rule, but you have to get an opportunity somewhere along the line," Dawson said. "In the five years that I was in the NFL, I started two games. I never started and finished a game, whether it be preseason or regular season. I never played two weeks in a row for any amount of time. In those days, the quarterbacks didn't get hurt."

The Texans moved to Kansas City and became the Chiefs in 1963. There, Dawson quarterbacked them into the first Super Bowl—a loss to the Green Bay Packers—and the fourth Super Bowl—a win over the Minnesota Vikings. He was named the Outstanding Player of Super Bowl IV and was startled to receive a call from President Richard Nixon after the game. It's thought to be the first time a U.S. president called to congratulate an athlete.

"He had called and talked to Hank Stram and he asked to talk to me," Dawson said. "Hank said, 'The president wants to talk to you.' And I said the president of what? President of the league? And he said, 'No, the president of the United States.' I said you've got to be kidding me. That was different."

Dawson retired in 1976 after 19 seasons. He was inducted into the Pro Football Hall of Fame in 1987. Did he ever think back to his time with the Steelers and gloat?

"No," he said. "It could've been easy to do that, but I was just grateful, really, to get the opportunity to play, to get an opportunity to prove to myself that I was good enough to play with these guys. That was the main thing. I felt I was very fortunate. I felt I was fortunate a guy like Hank Stram remembered me from college. The one piece of his puzzle he was looking for was a quarterback.

"See, the other coaches, Buddy Parker and Paul Brown, didn't know anything about the quarterback position, as far as the techniques. They never taught anybody anything. They may talk about the passing game and that, but I'm talking about the fundamentals of the position—the footwork, the ball-handling, all of that stuff. Bobby Layne was the worst. I don't think he ever threw a spiral. But Hank knew what he was doing."

Dawson entered broadcasting in 1966 as the sports director and anchor of a Kansas City TV station. By the time he retired from football, he had 10 years experience and began calling games for NBC Sports. In 1978 he joined HBO as an analyst for *Inside the NFL*. The next year he became co-host of the show with Nick Buoniconti and he remained in that position for 24 years.

Today, Dawson is sports anchor for KMBC-TV in Kansas City and color analyst on KCFX radio broadcasts of Chiefs games. He's also kept his sense of humor.

"I've been doing that for 21 years," he said. "So I've never had to work. I'm kind of like a writer. I've never really had a job."

CHAPTER 10

Jimmy
Orr

Jimmy Orr hasn't been this open since Super Bowl III.

"Wait," he said from his home in Brunswick, Georgia. "Let me fix myself a drink."

Wide open.

"Earl and I didn't talk about that play for 20 years," Orr said of the infamous flea-flicker that wasn't. Baltimore quarterback Earl Morrall didn't see Orr and instead threw to the other side of the field and the pass was intercepted by New York Jets safety Jim Hudson. The Jets beat the Colts in Super Bowl III as 17-point underdogs.

The play occurred with 25 seconds left in the half from the New York 42. The Colts were trailing 7-0, and Orr was wide, wide open, waving his arms near the goal line before the interception. Someone reported that Orr chewed Morrall out on the way to the locker room.

"Not true. Not true," Orr said. "We were like 50 yards apart and it was halftime, so I went in the locker room. No, I never yelled at Earl. He's much too nice a guy to yell at."

Orr and Morrall came together years later at a golf tournament that Orr and Mickey Mantle hosted. "He and I discussed it that night at the function, and that was 20 years after it happened," Orr said. "It was the first time we ever discussed it. It may have been more than 20 years. I can't remember."

And?

"He just said he didn't see me."

Frank Ryan saw Orr in an exhibition game against the Steelers in 1958 and launched a 72-yard bomb to the rookie for a Los Angeles Rams touchdown. Two days later, the Steelers traded a third-round pick (Tom Franckhauser) to the Rams for Orr and defensive lineman Billy Ray Smith.

JIMMY ORR
Seasons with Steelers: 1958-60
Position: wide receiver
Height: 5-foot-11
Playing weight: 185 pounds

"Harry Gilmer told me years later," Orr said, "that as I ran by Buddy Parker for that touchdown, Parker threw his clipboard on the ground and said, 'Hell, we'll never be able to trade for him now.' So apparently they had something working before then."

Smith moved into the Steelers' lineup next to Ernie Stautner at defensive tackle and Orr became the first Steelers Rookie of the Year. He caught 33 passes in 1958 for 910 yards and seven touchdowns. His average per reception was an absurd 27.6 yards, which stood as a career-high for a player who averaged 19.8 yards per catch throughout his 13-year career. Morrall was the Steelers' quarterback for the first two games in 1958, but he was traded to the Detroit Lions for Bobby Layne.

"Bobby and I hit it along pretty good," Orr said. "If you went out with him at night, he threw to you during the day. At that particular point in my life I could stand up to it. But it just worked out that way. I can't explain it. It was a great year, because, hell, I was borderline getting in the league anyway."

Orr was drafted by the Rams in the 25th round out of the University of Georgia, the 291st player selected. He's still the latest-drafted player ever to win the Associated Press Rookie of the Year Award. It took Layne to make the connection click.

"He was his own man," Orr said. "He called his own shots, and Buddy Parker let him do whatever he wanted to, so he did whatever he wanted to. But he could win. He called the game according to Parker. Parker put the game plan up there and Bobby memorized it. I don't think it was a hard thing for him to memorize—he was pretty damn smart—and he called the game plan just the way Parker wanted it. Parker might as well been out there on the field."

By the end of the 1958 season, the Steelers were red hot. They stunned the Chicago Bears, 24-10, when Orr made a spectacular juggling catch for a 48-yard touchdown to break a fourth-quarter tie. The Steelers went 6-0-1 in the second half of the season as Layne and Orr rewrote the Steelers' passing records.

"We were a ragtag bunch, believe me, but we wound up 7-4-1 that first year, which was pretty damn good for the talent we had," Orr said. "Buddy Parker was one helluva football coach. You have to give him credit for that. Buddy Parker never got his credit compared to the other coaches that I see around. He won two championships (Detroit in 1952 and 1953). He always had a competitive team, even in Pittsburgh when the talent was pretty thin. So Buddy Parker has not gotten his due out of the NFL in my opinion. I liked Buddy Parker and I thought he was a super coach. However, back in that stretch of time, Buddy wanted to trade and swap and do all that kind of stuff, and when you start doing that you're going to make some bad deals."

One of those appeared to be the trade of Orr after the 1960 season. The Steelers' momentum from 1958 had stalled. They didn't win more than six games in either of the next two seasons, so Orr was traded along with Joe Lewis and Dick Campbell to the Baltimore Colts for "Big Daddy" Lipscomb and center Buzz Nutter. Orr said the trade had to be made.

"I wouldn't go back," he said. "We had a lot of in-fighting, a lot of dissension within the team and so forth. It was just not worth going back. I would've quit, which I fully intended to do. In fact, I was down here where I'm living now when they called me and said, 'Would you play in Baltimore?' I said yes. Baltimore called back the next day and asked when I could be there. I ain't run a step, right? And this is in July. I said it'd take about a week to get in shape, and the general manager of Baltimore said, 'This ain't Pittsburgh. Be here tonight.'

"But there were a lot of problems in Pittsburgh; not like it is up there now. I think Dan Rooney is the reason. As much as I love Art Rooney, he wasn't that much into the pro football team. We were kind of a sideline and that was kind of the way it was run compared to the other NFL teams. If it wasn't for Buddy Parker, they couldn't have been representative back in the '50s and early '60s."

Orr never did get in shape in 1961, but he came back in 1962 to catch 55 passes to top Ray Berry (51) and backs Tom Matte (48) and Lenny Moore (27) as Johnny Unitas' preferred receiver.

The Colts added tight end John Mackey in 1963, and in 1964 they lost to the Cleveland Browns in the NFL championship game. The Colts reached the Super Bowl in 1968 and lost to the Jets. In 1970, after Orr lost his starting job to another ex-Steeler, Roy Jefferson, the Colts beat the Dallas Cowboys in Super Bowl V.

"I needed the ring because it was my last shot," Orr said. "They did ask me to come back the next year but I refused, because I told them I couldn't play the year before, so why would you want me to come back for another year? Hell, I couldn't play. I ran a 4.95. I mean, come on, you'd run a linebacker off at that speed, maybe even a lineman. I was beat up, hurt and so forth. If I thought I could've played, I would've gone back, but I knew I couldn't play."

Orr caught 400 passes in 13 NFL seasons, but he's best known for the catch he didn't make in Super Bowl III.

"Better to be known that way than not known at all," he said. "We beat Atlanta on the same play that didn't happen. It wasn't like it was something new."

In the second game of that 1968 season, in nearly the exact situation, Morrall lateraled to Matte, who lateraled back to Morrall who threw a 46-yard touchdown pass to Orr with 39 seconds left in the first half. It gave the Colts a 21-10 lead on their way to a 28-20 win over the Falcons.

"We had the same play in Pittsburgh and we called it a flea-flicker then, too," he said. "It goes back. Buddy Parker was as smart as any coach. He knew everything about offense."

After Orr stopped playing, he worked as a radio analyst for Falcons games. He quit when he was asked to become more critical of the team and soon thereafter became the Falcons' wide receivers coach (1975-77). When Orr stopped coaching, he moved to Las Vegas to work for a casino, which transferred him to Atlantic City.

"I moved over to the Sands about 1981, and one night Art Rooney came up there," Orr said. "I comped him into the gourmet room and he sent me two Steeler T-shirts and a letter thanking me for playing for the Steelers."

Orr was happy to see the Steelers win the Super Bowl after the 2005 season. He'd told friends in April 2004 that Ben Roethlisberger should've been the first or second pick of the draft. The win in Detroit validated that opinion.

"I'd seen him play a couple of games on Thursday night or something," Orr said. "One night it was windy as hell and the wind ain't affecting his ball. That was the night I said this guy can play.

"Unitas threw a great ball. It was soft and easy. It had a little hole in it, but in a 40-mile-an-hour wind? Whoa! Forget it. Like when we lost to Cleveland in the '64 championship game, there was no way. You probably wouldn't understand this, but when a guy throws a ball you can see a big hole or a little hole, depending on how tight the spiral is. There are four stripes in there and somehow or other you can tell whether they can cut the wind or not. That one night it was windy and that wind didn't affect Roethlisberger's ball.

"It's kind of like hitting a golf ball. If you hit a pure golf shot, the wind don't affect you, but if you hit it just a little bit off-center, you're done. So I was impressed with Roethlisberger. I still am. Obviously, if you win a Super Bowl the man's doing a pretty good job. Of course, he had a little help from the Georgia boy."

Is Orr a Hines Ward fan?

"Oh, yeah. He's wearing my number, too," said the Steelers' old No. 86. "So, yeah, I enjoyed that part of it. You enjoy being right."

CHAPTER 11

Myron Pottios

In his 12-year NFL career, Myron Pottios' job as middle linebacker was helped by the great lines he backed. In Los Angeles, he played behind the "Fearsome Foursome." And the gang he backed in Washington wasn't really over the hill. Pottios, though, would rank the line in Pittsburgh, particularly during his Pro Bowl rookie season, with either of the aforementioned.

"Look at that defensive line," Pottios said. "We had Ernie Stautner, Lou Michaels, Big Daddy, Joe Krupa. That's a good defensive line. Those guys were good ballplayers. You had a Hall of Famer in Stautner, and I think Big Daddy should be in the Hall of Fame. Lou and Joe were good ballplayers, too. Then on the outside you had [John] Reger. Overall our teams in '61 and '62 were pretty good teams. In '63 we played the Giants for the conference championship the last game of the year. That's when we had all those ties. We could've easily gone to the championship and played the Bears in '63."

Pottios could play a little bit himself. As a rookie out of Notre Dame in 1961, Pottios was called "the best rookie linebacker I've ever seen" by San Francisco 49ers coach Red Hickey, who'd been in the league since 1941. Pottios was a captain and All-America guard at Notre Dame. Prior to college he was considered the best high-school player in Pennsylvania—or at least one of the two best. The other was quarterback Dick Hoak, who led Jeannette to a 16-13 win over Pottios' Charleroi team in the 1956 WPIAL championship game.

The game-deciding play was a quarterback sneak by Hoak, who called for the ball from center when he saw Pottios back in pass defense 10 yards off the line. Hoak gained those 10 yards, then lateraled the ball away once Pottios grabbed him. The play was stopped at the 4-yard line, and Jeannette kicked a field goal to win at the gun. Four years later, the two marquee players were rookies with the Steelers.

Pottios was the second-round pick and an immediate hit on a team that had some talent. Prior to his second season, Pottios broke two bones in his arm

MYRON POTTIOS
Seasons with Steelers: 1961-65
Position: middle linebacker
Height: 6-foot-2
Playing weight: 232 pounds

and missed a 9-5 run by the Steelers. He returned in 1963, but Lipscomb didn't. He'd died of a heroin overdose the previous spring.

"He never received the publicity he should have," Pottios said. "Big Daddy was 6-7, 285 pounds, and he could run with the best. He was probably the fastest defensive lineman in football at the time, especially for that size."

The Steelers could've used Lipscomb in 1963. They ran neck and neck with the New York Giants for the Eastern Conference championship all the way to the final week of the season.

In a famous article that appeared in *True* magazine, author Myron Cope explained why the Steelers lost to the Giants, 33-17, at Yankee Stadium after beating them, 31-0, earlier in the season.

"It was not Y.A. Tittle's passing arm that hoisted the New York Giants," Cope wrote. "The Eastern race was, in fact, decided by a Pittsburgh quarterback's impetuous decision to go on the wagon."

Steelers quarterback Ed Brown, according to Cope, abstained from alcohol four days before the game. This behavior was not in keeping with the tradition set forth by the team Jim Brown had dubbed "the Gashouse Gang."

"He threw long, yards beyond his receivers," Cope wrote of Ed Brown. "His body well rested, his insides dry as a temperance union president's, his head disgustingly clear, he totally lost his timing and sangfroid. Time and again he overthrew receivers who had no one between them and the goal line. In short, Brownie had trained himself into the most miserable performance of his career."

Pottios remembered a different reason for the loss. "It was third down and 16," he said of a third-quarter defensive stand while the Giants held a 16-10 lead. "Gifford caught a pass that picked up 30 yards, then they scored and put the game away. I remember that play mostly. It was a tough catch, a one-handed catch on frozen ground. It was a great play on his part."

Pottios' next game was the Pro Bowl, and after the 1964 season he played in his third Pro Bowl in four seasons. His injury woes continued in 1965 when Pottios separated his shoulder in an exhibition game and played only six games. Coach Bill Austin traded Pottios to the Los Angeles Rams in the summer of 1966 for a 1968 third-round draft choice (K-WR Ken Hebert). The trade indicated a change in philosophy for the Steelers, who, under Parker, traded draft choices en masse for veterans. Pottios understood and agreed with Parker's philosophy.

"You can't go back and compare back then with today. It's altogether different," Pottios said. "You've got to understand, the players stay around Pittsburgh all year round now. They go to meetings and practices all year round, and they go over things. Back then, with the veterans, these guys knew the system and they were less likely to make mistakes. That's why at that point in time it was a good philosophy. Bring in the veterans because mistakes can cost you ballgames."

With the Rams, Pottios came under the spell of another practitioner of Parker's philosophy—George Allen. He became coach of the Rams in 1966 and traded for Pottios right away. In the next five years the Rams went 49-17-4 before Allen was fired and moved on to Washington.

Allen's biggest deal with the Redskins came on draft day 1971, when he made a trade that involved 15 players and draft picks. The Rams dealt Pottios, Jack Pardee, Diron Talbert, John Walker, Maxie Baughan, Jeff Jordan and a draft pick to Allen and the Redskins for Marlin McKeever and seven draft picks.

The Redskins became known as the "Ramskins," but after a few more trades they became known by the more familiar moniker of the "Over the Hill Gang." Within two years the Redskins played in Super Bowl VII, where they lost to the undefeated Miami Dolphins, 14-7.

Pottios collected his check from the game and bought a condominium in Palm Springs, California. He played one more season before retiring. He still lives in Palm Springs.

"Those were some good years at the end of my career," Pottios said. "In my career I played for Buddy and George Allen—two different type coaches but both were winners, but they were completely opposite in a way. George was an innovator and he would do anything he could to get an edge on the other team, whereas Buddy just wanted you to play football and go out there and do your job. We were successful with him, except for the '64 and '65 seasons."

At that point, Parker had lost patience with his players. Legend has it he once cut the entire team on a plane ride home.

"That's a true story," Pottios said. "It was on the way back from a game we lost. Buddy wasn't too happy. He had a tendency after the game to come back and walk up and down the plane and look at different individuals and tell them what he thought of their game, good, bad or indifferent. And sometimes, if he had a drink, he might get overboisterous. One time he was upset and he told one of the sportswriters that the whole team was fired, that he put us all on waivers. I seem to remember him saying 'You're all fired,' or 'You're all on waivers,' something along those lines."

After Pottios retired, he coached the Philadelphia Bell in the World Football League in 1974. The league folded and he left football and moved back to the west coast. He broke into the metals business and sold raw materials to the military and the aerospace industry. Pottios opened his own metals company in 1982 and remained in business until 1997.

"Now I'm in the title business—title insurance for homes," he said.

Pottios is married with a son and stepdaughter. Like many retired football players, he struggles with arthritis.

"When I was at the doctor the other day, he said, 'I've seen a lot of guys and you're a lot better than most,' so it's how you look at things," Pottios said.

When Pottios looks at things like a newspaper story about middling linebacker Julian Peterson signing a $54 million contract, he becomes upset—not at the player, but at the NFL Players Association for its settlement with the league in 2006.

"Nothing is included for the old players from '82 down," Pottios said. "I see most of the guys who need medical help and there's nothing there. All of us have arthritis, and as you get older it gets worse and worse. I was talking to Mike McCormack, who played with the Browns. He said there's nothing golden about the golden years of old football players. In our case it's gone downhill because of the health and the arthritis.

"We're trying to do something but we have to make more noise. We sat along the sideline too long and nobody got involved to get these guys to hear what the old-timers' problems were. Everybody talked about it, but nobody did anything; there weren't any committees set up. Now we're trying to get something going, but it might be too late. You never know. You've got to make a lot of noise and go out there and be seen and heard."

CHAPTER 12

Dick Hoak

Before Super Bowl XL, Dick Hoak worried about the mental state of Willie Parker, his inexperienced starting halfback.

"He might hyperventilate," said Hoak, the Steelers' running backs coach. "He hyperventilates in regular-season games sometimes. He didn't play in college, and now all of the sudden you're the starter in the Super Bowl. I'm sure it has to have some kind of effect on him."

Parker didn't know what to make of the statement, because, even by the end of his second season with the Steelers, he still didn't know what to make of Hoak.

"In my first year he used to yell at me; I don't think he liked me," Parker said. "Now he yells at me to let me know stuff hasn't changed, and he laughs about it. He's a funny guy, man."

Dick Hoak looks nothing like a funny guy. Perhaps that's what's given him the edge all these years. After 44 years with the Pittsburgh Steelers, Hoak likes to keep 'em guessing.

"I'm in this system to beat the system," he said. "They say that when you're hired in pro football as a coach, you're hired to be fired. Well I beat the system: I was hired, but I've never been fired. I may get fired, but that's the day I'll retire."

The Super Bowl marked the end of Hoak's 34th season as the Steelers' running backs coach. Hoak also served the Steelers as a player for 10 years. He took one year off after his playing days to coach highschool ball at Wheeling Catholic, but returned to coach running backs under Chuck Noll in 1972, the year the Steelers drafted Franco Harris. The running game has been a team—no, make that a city—staple ever since.

Hoak had been with the Steelers 44 years at Super Bowl XL. Bill Cowher, the NFL's longest-tenured head coach at 14 years, was 48 years old that day. Cowher was born six months after Hoak led his high-school team, Jeannette, to a WPIAL championship.

AP/WWP

DICK HOAK
Seasons with Steelers: 1961-70
Position: running back
Height: 5-foot-11
Playing weight: 195 pounds

Hoak and his wife, Lynn, live only a few miles away from Jeannette, in Greensburg, about 35 miles east of Pittsburgh. Hoak was born in a football town, educated in a football town, and works in a football town. In places like Jeannette, State College, and Pittsburgh, you're welcome only as long as you win, and Hoak has won.

At Penn State, Hoak played running back, defensive back, and alternated at quarterback with Galen Hall. As a senior, Hoak won the 1960 Liberty Bowl MVP award after running for two touchdowns, passing for one and intercepting a pass in a rout of Oregon.

Hoak was the second pick of the Steelers in 1961, but they had to wait until the seventh round to make the pick. The Steelers were winners at the time. The 1962 team went 9-5 and finished second in the Eastern Conference to the New

York Giants (12-2). The nine wins stood as a team record until 1972 (11-3).

The Steelers followed it up with a 7-4-3 record in 1963, one of Hoak's best seasons. He rushed for 679 yards and scored a career-high seven touchdowns. He should've had eight—and with it the Steelers would've had an 8-4-2 record—but for a quick whistle on an apparent touchdown run during the infamous 17-17 tie with the Chicago Bears, a game that was played less than 48 hours after the assassination of President John F. Kennedy.

"I remember sitting in a dressing room at Forbes Field, ready to go out on the field, when Bobby Layne and Tom Tracy came in and said that Ruby had just shot Oswald," Hoak said. "It was very strange."

And the stolen touchdown?

"I remember Ernie Stautner and Red Mack were chewing out George Halas, saying, 'You've got the officials in your pocket, George.'"

The Steelers finished the 1963 season on a strange 3-0-3 run, but their luck ran out soon thereafter. "From there, it was all downhill until I retired," Hoak said.

The Steelers won 24 games over the next seven years, mainly because Buddy Parker had bankrupted so many drafts, but Hoak did have a few highlights. He still holds the Hall of Fame Game record for longest completion: 80 yards to Gary Ballman in 1964. As a passing halfback, Hoak completed 20 of 40 passes for a career passer rating of 90.3. The passer rating of the Steelers' starting quarterbacks during Hoak's playing days (Ed Brown, Bill Nelson, Ron Smith, Kent Nix, Dick Shiner, Terry Hanratty, Terry Bradshaw) was 55.1.

Hoak's finest season as a runner was 1968, when he made the Pro Bowl after rushing for 858 yards (4.9 avg.). He retired after the 1970 season with 3,965 rushing yards. Hoak was the Steelers' No. 2 all-time leading rusher behind John Henry Johnson, and as of 2006 was fifth.

Hoak became Harris' rookie mentor when both joined the Steelers in 1972. Harris was the team's No. 1 draft pick, and Hoak replaced Max Coley as running backs coach. The team improved from 13th in the NFL in rushing to second that season. The team, of course, went on to win four championships by the end of the decade, and Harris ended up in the Hall of Fame.

The Steelers' running game reached its peak in 1976 when both Harris and Rocky Bleier rushed for over 1,000 yards, the only such achievement in team history. Both backs were injured in the divisional playoff win over the Baltimore Colts and couldn't play the following week when the Steelers lost to the Oakland Raiders in the AFC title game.

Harris was released before the 1984 season and Hoak coached team rushing leaders Frank Pollard, Earnest Jackson, Merril Hoge, and Tim Worley through the rest of the decade.

Noll retired in 1991, and Hoak wondered whether he was done as well, but Cowher was hired and he asked Hoak to become the only assistant holdover from Noll's staff.

It was a wise decision. With Hoak as his first lieutenant, Cowher's Steelers rushed for more yardage than any other NFL team the next 14 years. From 1992 to 2005, the Steelers rushed for 30,311 yards (4.1 avg.) and led the NFL in rushing three times (1994, 1997, 2001) behind team rushing leaders Barry Foster, Leroy Thompson, Erric Pegram, Jerome Bettis, Amos Zereoue, and Parker. The Steelers finished in the top five in rushing seven times and in the top 10 12 times. Bettis retired as the NFL's fifth all-time leading rusher with 13,662 yards, 10,571 of which were gained under Hoak and the Steelers.

Hoak was asked at Super Bowl XL how he coaches a player such as Bettis.

"My first year, after we saw what Franco could do in a preseason game, Coach Noll came over to me and said, 'Hey, don't overcoach him.' So that's what I do with Jerome. All I do is make sure we get the game plan. He knows the pass protections, knows the fronts, knows what he's supposed to do. I don't tell him where he should've cut or things like that. He knows. That's the other thing: I played the game and I could sit there as a coach and run that machine back and forth about four times and say, well you screwed up, you should've cut here or cut there, but that kid has that much time to make that decision. If you start second-guessing the running back, now you turn him into a robot and you have a mechanical player who's not worth a crap. He's thinking so much he doesn't know where to run. So I never do it with Jerome and I try not to do it with Willie."

Hoak had opportunities to coach elsewhere. When the USFL sprung up in 1982, he thought about jumping, but "I couldn't go across town and be in that other league and do that to Mr. Rooney.

"When Tony Dungy got hired at Tampa, Tony called me and wanted me to come there as a coordinator. I didn't do that. There was a time when the Philadelphia Eagles were looking for a coordinator and they asked for permission to talk to me, and I don't think they ever gave them permission. When George Perles left, he actually had the Indianapolis job and changed his mind and turned it down. He had wanted me to go there with him. I seriously thought about that one for a little while—about two hours.

"Yeah, I've had opportunities to leave. I couldn't think of leaving Mr. Rooney. When I was a player, he treated me very well. Some things happened when I was a player and he took care of me."

One example came about two-thirds of the way through Hoak's Pro Bowl 1968 season. He went to the Roosevelt Hotel to pick up his check and the Chief gave him a bonus.

"It was a check for a good bit of money," Hoak remembered. "He said, 'We stink, but you're having a great year and you deserve this.' So I left. And then in the last game of the year I dislocated my shoulder and I was going to the Pro Bowl. So I had to go to the doctors in Pittsburgh, which was right across the street from the Steeler office. I went in to say hello and Dan called me into his office. I went in there and he handed me another check. I told Dan his father had given me a check four or five weeks ago and he said, 'Yeah, I know.' They never had to do that, so I felt that they were loyal to me and that was one of the reasons, but it's not the only reason.

"My last year I got a concussion with two games left, and I spent a week or so in the hospital, and every morning and every evening Mr. Rooney would show up at that hospital. He'd bring me a paper in the morning and he'd come by in the evening to see if I needed anything. And he did that with all of us; he didn't just do that with me."

From Buddy Parker to Willie Parker, Hoak is the Steelers. He did some math one day and calculated that he "spent five years of my life in college dormitories just for damn training camps."

It's resulted in one of the greatest collections of jewelry in coaching history. Hoak has five Super Bowl rings. The late Bobb McKittrick also earned five as the offensive line coach of the San Francisco 49ers. The only coach with six is New England Patriots (and former Dallas Cowboys) strength coach Mike Woicik, but Hoak could end up on top yet.

"I might try to go until I'm 80," the 66-year-old said in 2006. "You're only as old as you feel."

CHAPTER 13

John Baker

When John Baker ran for sheriff of Wake County the first time, back home in Raleigh, North Carolina, he put the photo of the dazed and bloodied Y.A. Tittle on his campaign flyer with this message: "Baker sacked Y.A. Tittle and he'll sack crime the same way."

It worked. Baker won the 1978 election, and he won five more. He was sheriff for 24 years before losing to his political rival, Donnie Harrison, by less than one percent of the vote in 2002.

The two men will square off a third time in November, 2006. Each owns a victory against the other.

"It's just like football," Baker said. "If you don't win, you come back and work hard and come back strong. That's what I'm planning to do now."

Baker, 71, is a former all-star with the Steelers. He replaced Ernie Stautner at right defensive end in 1964, and the 6-foot-6, 270-pound Baker stayed there through 1967. Sacks weren't recorded in those days. Baker wishes they were.

"I would've been at the top of the list," he said.

Baker got Tittle good on September 20, 1964, at Pitt Stadium. Tittle was the 37-year-old quarterback of the defending NFL runner-up New York Giants. He was on his way to the Hall of Fame, and Baker hastened that arrival.

Tittle was rolling left, in search of Frank Gifford, when Baker blindsided him from the right. Baker's forearm knocked Tittle's helmet off, and the ball popped into the arms of Steelers rookie tackle Chuck Hinton. He returned it eight yards for a touchdown and a 27-24 Steelers win.

The picture of the bloodied Tittle, on his knees in the end zone, helmet off, gasping for air with broken ribs, is famous. But the sports editor of the *Pittsburgh Post-Gazette*, Al Abrams, chose not to run it. Photographer Morris Berman explained years later that the picture wasn't used, he was told, because Tittle was alone in the picture and the bleachers in the background were near empty.

AP/WWP

JOHN BAKER
Seasons with Steelers: 1963-67
Position: defensive end
Height: 6-foot-6
Playing weight: 280 pounds

Tittle retired after the season because of the rib injury, but Baker was into the prime of his career. Drafted out of North Carolina Central University by the Los Angeles Rams in the fifth round in 1958, Baker became a starter for the Rams at defensive tackle between Lamar Lundy and Lou Michaels. Baker was traded to the Philadelphia Eagles in 1962 for linebacker Bob Pelligrini.

Baker didn't work out with the Eagles. Coach Nick Skorich called Baker inconsistent and cut him at the 1962 camp. Baker didn't play until 1963, when he signed with the Steelers to replace Big Daddy Lipscomb. In 1964 Baker slid over to replace Stautner as the primary pass-rusher.

"I tried to pattern my career after Ernie," Baker said. "He spent a great deal of time with me, and I appreciate Ernie and respect him for that."

Baker was named second-team All-NFL by the *New York Daily News* in 1964. In 1965 he was voted team captain, but the Steelers were in steep decline from their perch as Eastern Conference contenders in 1963.

Mike Nixon became coach in 1965 and the Steelers went 2-12. Baker was named All-Eastern Conference by *The Sporting News*, but he didn't have much help. He anchored a line that included Hinton and Ben McGee, but middle linebacker Myron Pottios missed most of the season with a shoulder injury, and an injury to fullback John Henry Johnson crippled the offense.

Baker remained at right defensive end through 1967 and was traded to the Detroit Lions for linebacker Wally Hilgenberg, whom the Steelers cut. Hilgenberg was picked up by the Minnesota Vikings and spent the next 11 years as a member of "The Purple People Eaters." Baker went on to start 13 games for the Lions in 1968 and was cut at the 1969 training camp. That's when he moved into law enforcement full time.

Baker's father, John Sr., was a policeman and helped his son get a job with the North Carolina Prison Department in his first off-season home from the Rams. Baker Jr. remained in the field throughout his football career, and in 1978 became the first African-American sheriff in North Carolina since Reconstruction.

"Dad was on the force 40 years. He was the first African-American on the police force in North Carolina," Baker said. "His theory was that if you treat people like human beings, you're not going to have too much trouble. That was his belief, and that's my belief."

Baker encounters racism every now and then.

"I went into a part of the county shaking hands, and one individual looked at me and said, 'Your daddy was a good man, but I don't know you, and I won't vote for a nigger.' I said I hope you'll change your mind, but I wasn't going to argue with him. In the end I suspect he probably changed his mind, because I carried the municipality."

Baker became sympathetic to young detainees while working for the Prison Department. The more he met, the more he wanted to fix their environments. He became a rehabilitation worker for the Raleigh Police Department and went into the neighborhoods, schools, and homes. It's the part of the job that makes him want to return to work.

"When I lost the election by so few votes last time, I felt the citizens weren't dissatisfied with me or my administration," he said. "If I'd have lost by more that would've said to me, John, you need to go somewhere and sit down.

"It's just that every time I pick up the paper some young person has gone on the wrong side of law, and I'm not talking about minor transgressions; I'm talking about rape and murder. And I think I can help. I have 24 years of experience in the office. I have an athletic background. I know I can help. This is what drives me to go back into it."

Might he use some of that old Y.A. Tittle campaign magic?

"Someone just asked me that the other night," Baker said. "Y.A. came down and campaigned for me that first or second time I ran. He came down and spoke on my behalf, and I appreciated that, but of course time has moved on."

Baker's been married to Juanita since 1959. Their daughter, Jonnita, is a correctional examiner. Their son, John III, is a teacher and head basketball coach at Southeastern Raleigh High School. The team reached the second round of the big-school state playoffs in 2006.

Part of the school's athletic complex is named after John Baker Jr. He was voted into the North Carolina Sports Hall of Fame in 1972. Baker also keeps up with his favorite pro team.

"Nobody else but the Steelers," he said. "I was just as happy as they were when they won. The Steelers are my team and I will never deviate. The respect I have for Mr. [Art] Rooney will be forever. He was a good man. I used to talk to him and try to soak up that wisdom he had. He was just a good man.

"We stayed up late one night talking, and my wife got up the next morning and fixed him some grits, ham, red-eyed gravy, hot coffee, homemade preserves, and he said, 'I'm coming back.' That's the kind of owner he was. That's something I will always cherish."

Baker also has a message for Bill Cowher. The coach of the Steelers made the Raleigh newspapers early in 2006 when he bought a house in the area.

"Tell him if I win this election I'll make sure his family and his home are safe down here. I'll send a patrol car by there around the clock. He won't have anything to worry about."

CHAPTER 14

Bill Nelsen

Joe Greene and his wife happened into an Orlando golf shop one day, and Greene was recognized by one of the patrons, who asked Greene if he knew the shop's caretaker—former Steelers and Cleveland Browns quarterback Bill Nelsen. Greene said he did.

"Joe recognized me and told him I was the first guy he sacked," said Nelsen. "I said, 'Joe, you can't tell people those lies.' I asked him if he'd told his wife about the time he knocked my center's teeth out."

The two reminisced about their first meeting in 1969. Greene was a rookie defensive tackle and Nelsen was a 28-year-old quarterback for the Browns. The Browns beat the Steelers by 11 and then 21 points in 1969, but Nelsen took a worse beating in the second game. According to news accounts, Nelsen struggled to breathe as he told reporters of "those rookie animals on that defensive line." One of them, of course, was Greene.

"It was some good friends, too," Nelsen said 37 years later. "They chased me out of bounds one time when I threw an interception, and they didn't stop."

One of those "good friends" was Steelers linebacker Andy Russell, Nelsen's first roommate in the NFL. The two were drafted by the Steelers in 1963: Nelsen was a 10th-round pick out of Southern Cal and Russell was a 16th-round pick out of Missouri. It was a coup for the Steelers, considering they'd traded away their first seven picks. The Steelers also were lucky in that Nelsen could play quarterback.

"They drafted me as a defensive back," he said. "And I couldn't run very fast."

At USC, Nelsen alternated with Pete Beathard at quarterback for third-year Coach John McKay's 1962 national championship team. Beathard threw four touchdown passes in the Rose Bowl and was a highly touted junior. The Steelers had to be sold on Nelsen by west coast scout Fido Murphy.

BILL NELSEN
Seasons with Steelers: 1963-67
Position: quarterback
Height: 6 feet
Playing weight: 195 pounds

"He talked Buddy Parker into drafting me, and then they called Coach McKay and asked if I could do this and that. Coach McKay said, 'Well, he can play quarterback, but he's not going to play defensive back for you.'"

Nelsen proved McKay right when he starred at quarterback in the East-West All-American Game at Buffalo. As a rookie with the Steelers, Nelsen made two brief appearances. It wasn't until 1964 that Nelsen showed his potential. In the ninth game that season, Nelsen relieved starter Ed Brown at quarterback against the St. Louis Cardinals and directed fourth-quarter drives of 81 and 86 yards before falling short in a 34-30 loss.

Parker chose Nelsen to start the following week, but yanked him when the Washington Redskins went up by 13-0. Parker reinserted the young quarterback at 30-0 but didn't start him again.

Nelsen injured his right knee in the second exhibition game in 1965, leaving Parker to lean on the 36-year-old Brown. The night the Steelers lost an exhibition game to the San Francisco 49ers to fall to 0-4, Parker asked Dan Rooney to approve a trade that would send one of the Steelers' young defensive linemen—Ben McGee or Chuck Hinton—to the Philadelphia Eagles for veteran quarterback King Hill.

"We don't want to make trades in the middle of the night or after a team loses a ballgame," Rooney told Parker. "Let's wait until the morning."

Rooney went to see Parker the next morning, but the coach, who'd grown resentful of the emerging young executive power in the organization, turned in his resignation. Parker had done so on several previous occasions, but Rooney didn't talk Parker out of it this time. Rooney accepted Parker's resignation and promoted assistant Mike Nixon to head coach. Nixon announced that Nelsen would be his starting quarterback.

Problem: Nelsen was still injured. He hobbled through the 1965 season behind a porous offensive line and had his ups and downs. In October he threw three touchdown passes in a win over the Dallas Cowboys. In December he threw two interceptions against the Philadelphia Eagles and was yanked for Tommy Wade, who threw seven interceptions. It gave the team an NFL-record nine interceptions.

Bill Austin was Vince Lombardi's offensive line coach at Green Bay and became the Steelers' head coach in 1966. He planned to improve Nelsen's protection, but in the second game of the season that protection collapsed on Nelsen's other knee. He didn't return until three games were left in the season.

Of the five games Nelsen started in 1966, the 5-8-1 Steelers went 3-1-1. In the four games Nelsen started and finished, the Steelers averaged 40.3 points.

Nelsen opened the 1967 season where he left off: His first two completions extended his streak to 13 consecutive completions, which stood as a team record until Bubby Brister completed 15 in a row in 1989.

The Steelers didn't win much in 1967 as Nelsen struggled with another knee injury. The 27-year-old was traded to the Browns the following May, along with safety Jim Bradshaw, for quarterback Dick Shiner and defensive tackle Frank Parker. Both players came to Pittsburgh off serious leg injuries.

Newspapers reported that Nelsen had been at odds with Austin over who would do the play-calling. Nelsen said it was other things, like the infamous psychological tests Austin gave to players.

"He wanted to figure out if you had any goals and things like that," Nelsen said. "One question was: Do you want to kiss a girl, jump a 10-foot wall, or write a novel? Well, hell, I kissed the girl every time. So I had no goals. Bill Austin and I didn't agree on those kinds of things."

With a solid offensive wall in Cleveland, Nelsen missed only two games over the next four seasons. He threw for close to 10,000 yards in those four seasons and started the 1968 and 1969 NFL title games. Nelsen also quarterbacked the first televised *Monday Night Football* game. His opposing quarterback was Joe Namath, so Nelsen calls it "the no-knee bowl."

Nelsen also quarterbacked the Browns to four consecutive wins over the Steelers before the streak came to an end in 1970. That's when the Steelers beat the Browns 28-9 in the first game between the rivals at Three Rivers Stadium. Nelsen ran his record to 5-1 against the Steelers in 1971, but lost his final start against his old team in the return game in Pittsburgh, 26-9.

After that final start, Nelsen's old roommate, Russell, told reporters of a mid-week conversation he'd had with Nelsen. Russell said he'd warned Nelsen not to run around his end "because Dwight White and I will be waiting for you." Russell said that Nelsen's response was: "Dwight who?" This was relayed to White, a rookie defensive end, and he dominated the game.

"I do not remember saying anything close to that," Nelsen said. "I didn't want any of those animals coming after me."

Russell repeated the ploy two years later. Instead of Nelsen and White, the principals were San Diego Chargers quarterback John Unitas and Steelers tackle Ernie Holmes.

"Andy would do that; he's a University of Missouri guy," Nelsen said. "Ernie Holmes came when I was coaching at Tampa, and I tell you what, you didn't want to be around that guy. He'd kill you. I tried to put him to bed at curfew one night and he growled at me. I said uh, oh."

Nelsen retired after the 1972 season. He entered coaching and was an offensive assistant with New England (1973-74), Atlanta (1975-76), Tampa Bay (1976-82), and Detroit (1984). Nelsen said the highlight was coaching at Tampa Bay under McKay because Nelsen was McKay's first quarterback at USC. The pair guided the Buccaneers into the playoffs in three of Nelsen's last four years with the team.

"I also enjoyed developing the quarterbacks," Nelsen said. "I had [Jim] Plunkett, [Steve] Bartkowski, Doug Williams, and Gary Danielson."

Nelsen left coaching because he grew tired of moving his family. "I guess my pride got involved, too, because I got tired of calling people and asking for a job. It got old," he said.

Nelsen coached briefly at the University of Central Florida in Orlando before taking his current position at the golf shop.

"I've got great memories, tremendous memories of everything I've done in football," he said. "Unfortunately my body says I shouldn't have done all of that. The thrills of what I did playing and coaching keep me going, but both my knees hurt real bad; my neck and back and everything else hurt. I'm 65 going on 85."

Of his days with the Steelers, Nelsen said: "Most of my career at Pittsburgh was spent at Divine Providence Hospital on the North Side. Unfortunately I was hurt and the team wasn't real good."

Nelsen was one of the few players to have experienced the Pittsburgh-Cleveland rivalry as a starter in both cities.

"When I went to Cleveland it was a deal where you didn't win in Pittsburgh and I happened to win. I've got the picture from a game at Pitt Stadium of a fan holding a sign saying, 'Thank you Bill Austin for sending Bill Nelsen to Cleveland.' It was an exciting thing for me. But, yeah, they just got so much better. Chuck Noll came in and picked up the pieces with defensive people. The linebackers and the defensive line just made the difference with that team."

CHAPTER 15

Roy Jefferson

Chuck Noll's most impressive bit of coaching may have been the way he held the Steelers together after the 1-13 disaster in 1969.

"He was able to make them feel we were going someplace, that they should stay and be part of it," said Art Rooney Jr. "Only one guy wanted out."

That guy, Roy Jefferson, was the one star on offense. He was the NFL's third-leading receiver in 1969 but he was also flamboyant, hot-headed, and he wasn't shy about siding with teammates over management, as a team's player rep might. Jefferson was not—he wants to make clear—egotistical.

"I like Dan Rooney now," Jefferson said from his office in Annandale, Virginia. "He and I had our problems in negotiations, but I like Dan. I like Dan Rooney. Since I've left, there've been a couple times I've asked for favors and he didn't even think about it; last-minute stuff, too. I call and ask, and within two days I have it. I appreciate that. I appreciate him not holding anything against me because I was a hot-headed person, but I think in a sense rightfully so. As a young man that's how I chose to do it, but I probably wouldn't choose that way to confront them today. But I never, ever have been a person who was an egotist. I'm a team player. But I read a statement one time in a magazine that Dan thought that, because of Joe Greene and Terry Bradshaw, I wasn't going to be the focal point and that I would have a problem with that. God, that was the furthest thing from the truth.

"Hey, Dan's done a great job with that franchise, but he didn't know Roy Jefferson. He really did not know me. I have never been of that ilk. Never. I was a guy that wore flashy clothes and stuff like that, but like one of my old college teammates told me at our 40th reunion, there wasn't a guy on my college team that would ever say Roy Jefferson had to have the spotlight. There is not a one who would say that, and that's where you really go for the information: What was this guy like in college? I was a fun-loving, happy-go-lucky guy, but I was

69

AP/WWP

ROY JEFFERSON
Seasons with Steelers: 1965-69
Position: wide receiver
Height: 6-foot-2
Playing weight: 195 pounds

hot-headed. I didn't like being yelled at, cursed at. My mom told me at a young age that nobody needs to be cursing at you; just make sure you do what you're supposed to be doing."

Coming out of the University of Utah, Jefferson was tagged an "athlete" by scouts who didn't know where he should play. Jefferson was the WAC Player of the Year in 1964 when he played for the Redskins. That was the Utah nickname in the season they upset heavily favored West Virginia in the Liberty Bowl.

Jefferson was a running back, wide receiver, outside linebacker, defensive back, kick returner and place-kicker.

The Steelers drafted the 6-foot-2, 195-pounder in the second round in 1965 and weren't sure where to play him. "My first five, six, seven games I was going to both offensive and defensive meetings," Jefferson said.

Off the field, Jefferson loved Pittsburgh. He and his wife, Camille, and their infant son settled in Point Breeze, where "I knew people across Penn Avenue and back into Homewood, people within a mile or two of me," Jefferson said. "Here in Virginia, that never happened. It's just not that way. That is not the way here. So, people-wise, it was great, absolutely great."

And on the field? "On the field, we had terrible teams, but I didn't see it as terrible. I didn't see it as bad as it was. I don't know why. Our defense was a good defense. We weren't competitive offensively. That was our problem, but defensively we beat teams up—Ben McGee, Chuck Hinton, Ray May, Brady Keys. We had guys that came to play every day. Even offensively we had some parts, just not enough parts."

Jefferson caught 32 passes in 1966 and averaged 24.1 yards per catch. The numbers dipped to 29 and 15.8 in 1967, and after the season coach Bill Austin told Jefferson to prepare to play defensive back in 1968. At the first practice, Jefferson knocked three different men down on the first three plays.

"They were rookies who didn't know anything about running routes, and the coach got to yelling at me, he said, 'Jefferson, what the hell are you doing? You're supposed to be covering these guys.' I said he's not catching anything. I mean, I was covering him. He can't catch anything, can he? Oh, man, he got so pissed off."

The local newspapers reported that Austin and Jefferson had problems, but Jefferson said his coverage skills were not at the root of those problems.

"Austin and I had a problem because I overheard a conversation and I learned he was a racist," Jefferson said. "I overheard him talking to another racist in the league, the coach down in Atlanta, who I loved and rooted for growing up, Van Brocklin. I heard him talking to him between practices. I heard him mention his name. That's how I know who he was talking to. I overheard Austin say, 'I can't stand coaching some of them niggers, either.' When I heard that, it was over with. That's a statement I heard. It just, oh, God, he and I were at each other's throats from then on."

Jefferson got back at Van Brocklin with a record-setting day in November, 1968. Jefferson caught four touchdown passes in a 41-21 win. He caught 11 passes for 199 yards that day and finished second in the league that season with

58 receptions and 11 touchdown catches. He led the league with 1,074 receiving yards.

The next season, with Noll as coach, Jefferson finished third in the league with 67 catches and second with 1,079 yards. Even though he was the first Steelers receiver with back-to-back 1,000-yard seasons, Jefferson hadn't endeared himself to Noll, who sent the receiver home from Montreal during the 1969 exhibition season for missing curfew.

Jefferson was traded August 20, 1970, to the Baltimore Colts for receiver Willie Richardson and a fourth-round draft pick (Dwight White) in 1971. Jefferson said the blown curfew wasn't the reason for the trade. "We brushed up in training camp," Jefferson said. "A bunch of receivers were hurt, and the doctor told me not to practice because I had some kind of cold or something. I told the doc I was fine and could practice, but he wouldn't let me. I insisted, but so did he, and so I stayed out. But when it got to the passing drills, there were only two receivers who could run, and there were back-to-back passing drills that were like 20 minutes or so in 95-degree heat and 90 (percent) humidity. These kids were rookies and they were running. I went over to the receivers coach, Lionel Taylor, while the receiver, Hubie Bryant, and the other kid kept running. They were running all out on every play. I told Lionel he should tell the coach to have one of them at least shut down on a play so just the hot side would run. Well, I didn't see Lionel tell him, so I just went out changing with the receiver who was not the hot receiver, and I'd run the pattern so the other guy could rest. And then, oh, about 10 minutes in, this quarterback, Hanratty, throws me the ball on the off side. I said what the hell, but I caught the ball, and Noll saw it. 'God damn it, Jefferson. You're not supposed to doing anything. Get your ass off the field.' I didn't like people cursing at me, and I gave him a few expletives and went out. But nobody there, except Lionel Taylor, knew what I was doing. I wasn't screwing up. I was trying to help somebody.

"So I went into the locker room and they brought Bryant in and he was packed in ice. They brought him into the training room and an ambulance came and took him to the hospital. The kid almost died. So Coach called me in after that and he told me he was getting tired of me usurping his authority and all this. I said, 'Coach, I thought you were a fair person, but you're not a fair person. You had two receivers running back-to-back passing drills in 95 degree heat, 90 humidity, and a kid almost died out there today, and you're up here talking to me about my attitude when all I wanted to do was give them a break so they didn't kill themselves.' Then I swore at him and told him he could kiss my behind. I said I could care less about playing for him anymore. Trade me, please, because I don't want to be a part of anything that you're involved with.

"So that probably did it."

Probably. There was also that matter of Jefferson, the player rep, solidifying the players during a brief league strike in camp that year.

"I was talking to the *Pittsburgh Press* reporter, Pat Livingston, at St. Vincent," Jefferson said. "He was interviewing me and I was with Joe Greene and L.C. Greenwood, and I got on him about his reporting. I said you've never even asked me about the strike and what we wanted. I said you're only giving the owners' side. You get to ride on the plane and everything, but you're doing an injustice to the rest of the fans by not telling both sides of the story.

"I was all on him about that, and he actually was a little upset about it. I didn't realize it but Joe Greene was getting incensed about it, too, and all of the sudden he hockered up and spit in Pat Livingston's face, right on his eyeglasses and stuff. But when the paper came out the next day, you'd have thought Roy Jefferson spit in his face. That's how bad it was. I don't know, somebody told somebody something. He knew who did it, but you would've thought I spit in his face the way the article was written. I couldn't believe it."

Less than a month later, Jefferson was traded.

"I don't regret any of it," he said. "I went to Baltimore and we won a Super Bowl there the next year, and then I went to the Redskins and we went to the Super Bowl two years after that and went to the playoffs every year. I wasn't a part of four Super Bowls, but I wouldn't have been anyway based on the timing of my career."

Jefferson retired after the 1976 season and continued to serve the players' union. In a 1982 interview during a strike, Jefferson explained why the players deserved 55 percent of the revenue. They didn't get it—until the next decade. And in 2006, the players secured 59.5 percent of the league revenues.

Jefferson works for several charities in the Washington, D.C. area. He's been in the restaurant business (Jefferson BBQ I, II and III), made a movie (*Brotherhood of Death* in 1976), works in the title insurance business full-time and part-time as a broker, is still married to Camille—or Candy as she's better known—and has three children and two grandchildren. He also has a legacy as one of the true free spirits in the NFL.

"You might say," Jefferson said with a chuckle. "I came with a flair. I enjoyed myself."

CHAPTER 16

Bruce Van Dyke

Back before Tunch and Wolf there were Moosie and The Old Ranger. Bruce "Moose" Van Dyke and Ray "Ranger" Mansfield were the Tunch Ilkin and Craig Wolfley of the early 1970s. Not that the two conquered radio, but Moosie and the Ranger came to life in the bestselling book at the time, Roy Blount, Jr.'s *Three Bricks Shy of a Load.* The book chronicled the 1973 season, and Van Dyke and Mansfield were the stars.

"You think?" asked Van Dyke 33 years later. "I never thought of it that way."

Van Dyke was the right guard, and the late Mansfield was the center in those Bill Austin-to-Chuck Noll transition days. *Sports Illustrated* dispatched Blount to chronicle this dynasty-in-the-making, and the best, most honest chapter was a transcript of a training-camp conversation between Van Dyke and Mansfield. Their topics bounced from the Steelerettes to hurting opponents to cheapshot artists to frauds to Curly Culp and to Dick Butkus. It took up the full chapter. The two showed the humor you'd find *In the Locker Room,* and more. At one point Blount wrote of Van Dyke: "Of all the Steelers, he may have been the most thoroughly reflective."

"Are you sure it said that?" Van Dyke said with a laugh. "I read that so long ago. I guess there was a time when I was in my prime."

So how does Van Dyke look back on those days with the Steelers?

He paused.

"I'm afraid I'm not going to be very reflective or interesting," he said.

But there's this: Van Dyke was traded by the Pittsburgh Steelers to the Green Bay Packers in September, 1974. In effect, Van Dyke played for the '60s Steelers and the '70s Packers.

"It was just one of those things that happened," he said. "Sure, you wished you would've been on those teams, but I wasn't. The thing of it is, though, it was

BRUCE VAN DYKE
Seasons with Steelers: 1967-73
Position: offensive guard
Height: 6-foot-2
Playing weight: 255 pounds

such a great experience being with the Steelers, from the point of coming from that 1-13 team to winning our division. That was very gratifying in itself.

"The toughest thing about being traded like that is we were just on the verge of, well, winning the Super Bowl; but there's a difference in being on a winning team like that where you're expected to win and going to a team where you know you don't really have a chance and the whole atmosphere is negative. It was quite a letdown, but what are you going to do? That's my buddy Dan Devine."

Devine coached Van Dyke, and earlier Andy Russell, at Missouri and sought both players when he became coach of the Packers. Russell came out of Missouri in 1963, and Van Dyke came out in 1966. Van Dyke was drafted in the 12th round by the Philadelphia Eagles and was traded the next year, along with fullback Earl Gros, to the Steelers for wide receiver Gary Ballman. Van Dyke played two years under Austin, and the Steelers won a combined six games. Noll was hired in 1969, but Van Dyke didn't sense an immediate about-face.

"Not at first," he said. "We liked Chuck for the fact he was a hands-on coach and he knew all the techniques of all the players and was a real student. Of course, we didn't know what was down the road. I don't know, we just kind of lived it with the fans. Joe Greene was drafted, and we started getting pretty good. Then all those other guys came along, and the rest is history."

Greene held out for 23 days after the Steelers made him the No. 1 pick in the 1969 draft. This didn't sit well with the veterans, and Van Dyke and Mansfield wanted to prove that point.

"We were veterans and he was a rookie," Van Dyke said. "And of course he was getting all of this play and everything, and we were going to teach him a lesson. After all it was two against one, so basically I'd take him and Ray would try to cut him. That didn't seem to work too well. He had such strength; it was unbelievable what kind of strength he had. He could actually carry both of us, split us and carry both of us back to the quarterback. He made believers out of us right away."

But the Steelers went 1-13 that year. Same old Steelers?

"It was pretty miserable before Chuck came," Van Dyke said. "I mean, we still had a good time, but the difference was like night and day. I remember we played at Pitt and we had like 19,000 people come to see us, and by halftime there'd be 6,000 or so in the stands. Then all of the sudden you started winning and you're introduced at a stadium, everyone's pounding their feet at Three Rivers, making a roar. It made a difference."

Three Rivers Stadium opened in 1970, the year the Steelers drafted Terry Bradshaw, Ron Shanklin, and Mel Blount. In 1971 they drafted Frank Lewis, Jack Ham, Dwight White, Larry Brown, Ernie Holmes, Mike Wagner, and Van Dyke's eventual replacement, Gerry Mullins. In 1972 they drafted Franco Harris, and the running game began to click.

Harris became the NFL Rookie of the Year and he called Van Dyke and Sam Davis "the best guards in the league." When Van Dyke and Davis both missed the same two games in December, Harris averaged only 3.2 yards per carry. Before that, he'd averaged 5.5 yards per carry.

After the season, Van Dyke was named to a smattering of all-star teams. He played his best game against Cincinnati in early November. The Steelers rushed for 230 yards in a 48-17 win, and Van Dyke was named NFL Offensive Player of the Week. Reporters noted one play in which Van Dyke pulled to block a linebacker and then, while crawling, blocked a defensive back to spring Harris for a 21-yard run.

"We were doing so well, they were running out of people to give the award to, so they had to give it to me," Van Dyke said. "But I do remember it was the Cincinnati game. I always went against Mike Reid, and I always got more psyched up to go against him than anybody else. And I did have a good game, but I think it was more a case where somebody up there was rooting for me and stuck my name in there. But, yeah, it was quite an honor. It was probably one of the greatest things that ever happened to me."

Van Dyke was named to the Pro Bowl after the 1973 season. He was the only Steelers offensive lineman named to the Pro Bowl during a time span framed by Charley Bradshaw in 1963 and Mike Webster in 1978. Van Dyke was the only Steelers guard to make the Pro Bowl in a 31-year stretch between John Nisby in 1961 and Carlton Haselrig in 1992. It was clear that Van Dyke had plenty to do with the Steelers' success running the ball.

"I'd like to think so, but I think a lot of it had to do with the fact that Chuck Noll came up with some base counter plays and traps," he said. "We were a small line, and we got very good running with Franco, Frenchy, Preston Pearson, Rocky. We as a team became very good at running these traps, and we had variations off the same traps and the same counters that confused the defensive guys. I was the guy who pulled on a majority of plays, so I was the guy everybody saw. A lot of times I'd be able to take the guy I was blocking—the defensive end or linebacker—by surprise because he doesn't know exactly who's going to get him. Say Rocky's running at the end and the linebacker, and I'd be coming around the other way. They'd sometimes get confused as to which of us was going to get him and I'd be able to blind-side a guy. It showed up on film because Franco was right behind me. So, yeah, maybe I looked pretty important, but it was probably more a case of being in the right place at the right time."

Van Dyke and Harris played with injuries in 1973, and the running game slipped to eighth in the league. The team bounced back in 1974, but Van Dyke missed the exhibition games with calf trouble, and even saw his iron-man streak at the 19th Hole come to an end because of it. The Steelers were 6-0 in the preseason and bursting with confidence when they traded Van Dyke to the Green Bay Packers the Monday before the opener of their first Super Bowl season. Devine, who felt he was being undermined and wanted more of "his guys" around him in Green Bay, traded a third-round pick in 1976 (Penn State DT Ron Coder) to the Steelers.

Van Dyke played one game in 1974 and then two full seasons before retiring. Green Bay won six, four, and five games in 1974, 1975, and 1976.

At the age of 32, Van Dyke made more money in a coal mine he co-owned in Uniontown, but that's when times were good. Van Dyke got out of the business, he said, because "all the little guys got driven out by the big, low-priced longwall operators and consolidators."

Through the connections he'd made, Van Dyke moved into his current position as sales manager for a stone quarry and asphalt plant in Uniontown.

"I've got a 16-year-old that I've got to get through college yet," said the father of three and grandfather of four [with a fifth on the way] from his home in nearby Peters Township.

"I'm a ways from retiring yet. I think I'll have to use my social security to pay for his college, but I enjoy what I'm doing and I'll probably do it for several more years."

ver the center's head. The "odd 4-3" was first used as a passing-downs
nt in weeks five through 12 in 1974, and in week 13 at New England it
d on a third of the snaps.

he Steelers did it for two reasons: 1.) Middle linebacker Jack Lambert
t back and read plays with less intrusion from offensive linemen; and 2.)
was bored one day in practice and gave it a try.

What makes it work so well is Greene's speed and quickness," Perles said
ime.

the final game of the regular season, the alignment, which came to be
as the "stunt 4-3," was used to wax Cincinnati, 27-3. In the playoffs the
' stunt 4-3 defense dominated all three games. In a first-round win over
falo Bills, the Steelers held Simpson to 49 yards rushing. In three playoff
combined, the Steelers allowed 99 yards rushing. They stuffed the
d Raiders, 24-13, before setting defensive records in a 16-6 win over the
ota Vikings in the Super Bowl. Dwight White stepped out of a hospital
h pneumonia that day to play one of his best games, but Greene was the
r in the middle.

oe was the single best football player down the stretch this year that I've
n," said Carson.

Greene played during the playoffs better than any defensive lineman I've
n," said Noll.

t the age of 28, Greene was at the peak of his career, but he pinched a
n his neck on November 2, 1975 against Cincinnati and was never the
He returned that season to play against the Raiders in the playoffs, and
lit time with Steve Furness in Super Bowl X, a 21-17 Steelers win over
wboys. Rumors circulated at the time that Greene was injured during a
ith Lambert, and that Lambert had scored a decisive victory.

ambert and Noll were asked about the rumor at the time and both
d it off as preposterous. "You ought to keep spreading that one around,"
used Lambert told the reporter. Greene dismissed the rumor with a smile
asked about it more than 30 years later.

I just slipped while I was warming up for the game," he said. "Yeah, I was
rent player after that. I probably wasn't quite as agile as I had been before.
d a different style of game. I only participated in one Super Bowl when I
althy."

Greene was named to the Pro Bowl in 10 of his 13 seasons and was
ed into the Hall of Fame in 1987. He was voted the Steelers' all-time
t player by fans in a 2000 vote. The Steelers' Rookie of the Year award is

CHAPTER 17

Joe Greene

Joe Greene didn't come up with the slogan "One for the Thumb." He was just the first one to use it. And it hung on the big guy like an albatross until he finally won that fifth ring. Greene won One for the Thumb as a member of the 2005 Steelers.

So how did it feel, Mean Joe? How did it feel to finally win One for the Thumb?

"That's all utter nonsense," said Greene. "It's one for the right hand. It's one for *this* group, for *this* team."

Greene was shouting by now, and maybe he had a right to. It had been 25 years since Greene uttered the slogan at a marketing event, but it fit so well that it eventually became an embarrassment that had to be excised—for the sake of *this* group, for *this* team.

Greene works in the personnel department for the Steelers. He made the career move in 2004 and helped the Steelers draft Ben Roethlisberger. Of course, Roethlisberger was a lucky break, but the rest of the weekend wasn't so easy. An exhausted Greene plopped into a chair at the end of it. "I can't say it's easy by any means," he said.

Greene didn't work this hard on draft day 1969. Dan Rooney did all the heavy lifting then. First, Rooney announced the hiring of Chuck Noll. Rooney made sure the new coach was hooked up for a conference call with the media before Noll was to leave for the draft later that afternoon.

One of the first questions put to Noll that morning was whether he'd draft local native Terry Hanratty in the first round. O.J. Simpson hoped to be drafted by the Steelers because former USC teammates Ray May and Mike Taylor were with the team, but Simpson was the hands-down No. 1 pick, so fans and reporters figured Hanratty, the Notre Dame quarterback from the Pittsburgh suburb of Butler, would be available with the fourth pick.

Noll, on the phone from Baltimore, where he'd
defensive coordinator with the Colts, told the reporter th
long to develop and that the Steelers needed immediat
pointed out the records of the Steelers, Pirates, Penguin
told Noll, "this is the City of Losers."

"We'll change history," Noll said, and a few hours
Greene in the first round. Hanratty lasted until the sec
knee problem.

Noll had scouted Greene during his junior and
Texas State. The 6-5, 275-pound Greene anchored a lir
per carry, but Noll liked Greene's pass rush even better.

"Pass defense begins with the rush on the passer,"
is a big, strong, tough boy who wants to play real bad."

The only problem was that Greene didn't wa
Pittsburgh.

"It should've been the happiest day of my life, I
about it," Greene said. He held out for 23 days, and
season he wished he'd held out longer.

"Miserable, miserable, miserable, miserable," wa
the season. Greene even picked up a nickname he despi
from a combination of his college's nickname—the M
that Greene was, well, mean. He was ejected from two
and once picked up a football and heaved it into the
Franklin Field. In his second training camp, Greene
sportswriter Pat Livingston and, after discussing the n
he'd do it again.

On the field, Greene was being called the most ir
in the league, and his surliness figured to be a result
Steelers didn't begin winning with consistency until the
close loss to the Dallas Cowboys, the Steelers won fiv
ended the season in the playoffs.

"Now I wouldn't want to be on another team," G
Times. "This is history happening." Just as Noll had
Greene the catalyst.

Greene was the centerpiece of the "Steel Curtain"
named Defensive Player of the Year by all three of the m
in 1972. Greene won the award again in 1974. He do
line coach George Perles and coordinator Bud Carson

JOE GREENE
Seasons with Steelers: 1969-81
Position: defensive tackle
Height: 6-foot-4
Playing weight: 275 pounds

called the Joe Greene Great Performance Award, but perhaps Greene's greatest honor came in 2000, when Rooney asked Greene to present him into the Hall of Fame.

"I was flabbergasted," Greene said.

After his retirement, Greene bought a restaurant in Dallas and worked as a color analyst for CBS-TV. He joined Noll's staff as a defensive line coach in 1987 and remained with the team until Noll resigned in 1992. Greene interviewed for Noll's old job, but the Steelers instead hired Bill Cowher, so Greene went to Miami to coach Don Shula's defensive line. He held the same position in Arizona four years later before switching gears with his career. In 2004, Greene became a special assistant in the Steelers' personnel department. Greene scouts both pro and college prospects for director of football operations Kevin Colbert.

"The Steelers have been in my blood for many, many years, since the beginning," Greene said. "When I went to work elsewhere, I put those groups in the forefront, but the Steeler blood was still in me. The interest in what was going on in terms of the won-loss record for the Steelers was always there. My concentration and my dedication to what was at hand was with the people that I was working for, but my loyalties never wavered."

As for scouting, Greene says he's not really doing anything new.

"I've been scouting since the day I got drafted by the Steelers," he said. "We came here 1-13 and so I followed the draft in the papers. I called everybody because we were looking to get some help. All that time, from playing to coaching, it's players that allow you to win."

CHAPTER 18

Frenchy Fuqua

The Frenchman dresses more conservatively these days. How could he not? The running back who wore capes and carried gold canes and walked on glass heels filled with live goldfish now takes more pride in his health and vitality.

"I had prostate cancer three years ago, and I'm currently cancer free," he said. "I played in 1970 at 206 and now I weigh 199, and I still try to pump a little iron. And I haven't got any gray hair on my head. I want you to write that."

That was the ace John "Frenchy" Fuqua had up his sleeve when the Detroit native hosted the world the week his Steelers played in Super Bowl XL. Frenchy went to the parties and toasted the old boys; he went to the game and toasted the new boys.

"I'm still recuperating from it," he said. "I'm getting too old. I haven't partied and had a chance to see that many people in a long time, but it was just fantastic. And I told the guys, especially Andy Russell, they had to do something with all that gray hair."

Fuqua was the halfback next to Franco Harris until the middle of 1974, when an injury opened the door for Rocky Bleier. Fuqua's claim to everlasting fame, though, is the Immaculate Reception. He was the intended receiver of a pass that was going nowhere, but Fuqua collided with Jack Tatum and a dynasty popped into the air.

So, what about it Frenchy? What about the Immaculate Reception? Did you touch it?

"All I can tell you is that it was immaculate," he said with a laugh.

It's the greatest play in NFL history. The Raiders contend it's the greatest heist in NFL history. They argue the ball hit Fuqua at the Oakland 35, where he, Tatum, and the ball intersected before it bounced back to Harris. Back in 1972, two offensive players couldn't touch a forward pass. Fuqua declined comment after the game, just as he declines comment today.

"People have tried everything to get it out of me," he said. "Most say, 'I'm going to buy you beer until you tell me,' but what happens is they wind up telling me their life story before we're done.

"I don't know. It really goes back to a promise I made to the Chief years and years ago. At the time I planned to tell the story, but it became a lot more intimate to me when I lost him. The first 10 years went by and I hadn't told anybody, then 15 years, then I started getting offered money, and I passed up some pretty good deals as a matter of fact. If there's anything the Frenchman's going to hold in his heart, and hold to his word, that's what it is. And every anniversary Franco and I call each other up to wish each other happy anniversary."

Fuqua said the Chief "made the NFL experience for me." Fuqua was traded by the New York Giants to the Steelers, along with middle linebacker Henry Davis, for quarterback Dick Shiner on April 30, 1970. That's when Fuqua went from owner Wellington Mara to Rooney.

"They were probably two of the most impressive and loving and God-fearing men on this planet," Fuqua said. "Mr. Rooney was just a quiet guy with a cigar, but when he spoke to you it was like a word from the wise. He never said anything bad to you, and even when no one in that locker room would speak to you after a bad game the Chief would come up and say something nice and that would make you want to try that much harder the next Sunday."

Fuqua set a team record in the 1970 finale by rushing for 218 yards against the Philadelphia Eagles. He ripped off a 72-yard touchdown run on the Steelers' first play, and later ran 85 yards on a trap sprung by right guard Bruce Van Dyke and left tackle Jon Kolb. The total was the best in the NFL that season and remains a Steelers record. Fuqua said he went into the game with back spasms and team doctors tried to persuade him not to play.

"They put all this hot stuff on my back and wrapped me up. I went through the pregame workouts and kept moving because I couldn't let it stiffen up on me. The first play of the game I went for a long touchdown and I said wow, it felt good, didn't hurt. I came to the sideline and [Ralph] Berlin said, 'I'm a great trainer, aren't I?' I laughed and I kicked up and down the sideline, went back out there and stayed active.

"The great temperature—it might've been closer to 70—that day was a factor. And I remember on the next big run I broke through the line and got frightened because there wasn't nothing but daylight in front of me. Now, I'm not the fastest guy, but I'm proud of the fact that once I'm in the clear I've never been caught from behind. I just took off for the end zone."

AP/WWP

FRENCHY FUQUA
Seasons with Steelers: 1970-76
Position: running back
Height: 5-foot-11
Playing weight: 205 pounds

It's the third-longest run in team history. The Steelers haven't had a 200-yard rusher since.

"I thought my guy Willie Parker was going to break it this year," Fuqua said. "Before him, I thought Barry Foster would break it."

Fuqua is also remembered for his outrageous outfits, which he said were encouraged by the Chief.

"I'd say here's what I'm going to wear this coming Sunday. He'd say, 'What is it Frenchy?' And I'd tell him, well, I'm going to have a musketeer hat and this and that and he'd say, 'Well I think you look grand. Knock 'em out kid.' And that was the OK I needed. As long as I got the OK from the Chief I knew I'd knock everyone out that Sunday."

Fuqua's boldest outfits included glass heels with the goldfish. He'd met a manufacturer during a Dapper Dan banquet, but the man lost Fuqua's number.

"I got home from practice one night, and I'm in the bathroom and my wife at that time said, 'Frenchy, they're talking about you on TV. Come in here.' The man had sent four pairs to the station and they said, 'Frenchy, you've really outdone yourself this time. Come on down and get them.' That's how it started off, but there was one thing: They were 10 1/2 and I wore a size 11 triple E. I had a wide foot and they killed me. The first time I wore them they were great, but after 40 minutes my feet were killing me. So I wouldn't wear them until I got to wherever I was speaking, and it worked well, except if I was out for an hour the fish would die. There wasn't enough water. I had all type of people come up with ideas and they never worked. I tried hoses in my pants. I put tubes down there. Nothing worked."

These days, Fuqua wears a more conservative shoe. He's worked in the Detroit newspaper business as a circulation manger since he retired from the game.

"I tried to hang on all the way till my 40s," he said. "But eventually I started busting out of them, or the zipper wouldn't come up, and I couldn't stand the boys laughing at me a couple of times, so I just said OK, and slowly but surely my tastes became more conservative."

Fuqua led the Steelers in rushing in 1970 (691) and 1971 (625) and tied Ron Shanklin for the team lead with 49 receptions in 1971. He was leading the team in rushing in the second half of the 1973 season when he broke his collarbone. Fuqua lost his job for good in November, 1974 when he broke his wrist and was replaced by Bleier. Fuqua was a spot starter in 1975 and 1976 and retired after spending 1977 on injured reserve.

Noll kept Fuqua as long as he could because of his versatility. Fuqua could play both running back positions and had great hands, which had been a weakness.

"We were a small black college in Baltimore [Morgan State] that ran the ball 95 percent of the time," he said. "When I thought I might have an opportunity to come to the NFL, I talked to an alumnus and he told me to get silly putty, work it, go to bed with it, work it in both hands, and at night before bed throw the ball up 100 times and catch it. That guy was Leroy Kelly."

It's a trick Fuqua shared with his son, Derrion, who was Wayne State's defensive MVP as a cornerback in 2005. Fuqua also has a daughter, Keylea, and sons Ryan and John. Ryan was a star running back at Wesley College in the early 1990s, and John played strong safety at Louisville until tearing up his knee as a senior.

Fuqua and his wife, Shree, planned to retire to Florida in 2006, three years after he learned he had prostate cancer.

"I'm kind of a health fanatic, so I'd been getting my prostate checked since I was 47," he said.

At the age of 56, Fuqua tried to skip the exam. It was cold and snowy and he was looking for an excuse to head to Florida early. Someone talked him into taking the extra few minutes with the doctor.

"I had a little spot," he said. "We caught it early and had it removed. Two weeks later they had another scan, and that was probably the most trying time I've had in my life. I pulled through it, and three years later I only have to go once a year. I look back on it and I just push it to everyone: Get checked once a year. Start off now."

CHAPTER 19

Frank Lewis

A Louisiana newspaper columnist wrote that Frank Lewis would've been inducted into the state's Sports Hall of Fame a lot sooner had he been a little more flashy or flamboyant. Bill Nunn said the same thing about Lewis when he was with the Steelers.

Nunn is the Steelers scout who stalked the country's small black colleges in the late 1960s and early 1970s. He found Lewis at Grambling and believes Lewis would've been remembered as the Steelers' greatest wide receiver had he been more assertive with quarterback Terry Bradshaw.

"I wasn't into playing politics," said Lewis. "If I had been, I probably would've gotten more attempts, because that's what it's all about: The quarterback's got to give you attempts to make catches and plays."

In 13 NFL seasons, Lewis made plenty of catches and plays, but the majority of his 397 catches came in his six seasons with the Buffalo Bills. Lewis was traded by the Steelers to the Bills for gout-riddled tight end Paul Seymour in 1978. Seymour failed his physical and was sent back to the Bills. Lewis, meanwhile, broke out of the shadows cast by Lynn Swann and John Stallworth to put up the five best reception totals and six best yardage totals of his pro career. Lewis made the Pro Bowl after the 1981 season, when he caught 70 passes for 1,244 yards.

The trade ranks as one of Chuck Noll's worst.

"Even in Buffalo I wasn't the featured receiver," Lewis said from his home in Houma, Louisiana. "We had Jerry Butler and he was the featured receiver. I just happened to be in a good system where they spread it around a little bit. In Pittsburgh we were hard-nosed, ran the ball, and threw seldom. And Bradshaw tended to lean one way. He favored the right side, where Swann played and, before him, where Ron Shanklin played.

AP/WWP

FRANK LEWIS
Seasons with Steelers: 1971-77
Position: wide receiver
Height: 6-foot-1
Playing weight: 196 pounds

"Terry was effective and did a good job. We won, and his team was successful and won Super Bowls, so how can you complain? But like Mr. Nunn said, looking back now I would've asked for the ball a little more, no doubt."

Lewis grew up in southern Louisiana as a basketball player, but in his only high school football season averaged six yards per carry as a fullback and led South Down High in interceptions. He went to Grambling and played wingback in Coach Eddie Robinson's wing-T offense. Lewis averaged 10.8 yards per carry and was quarterback James Harris' favorite receiver as a junior and senior.

"Coach Rob used to run pass patterns in practice to show you how to do it," Lewis said of the legendary Grambling coach. "You'd have to run the route while he was pulling your arm and guiding you. He was a great coach, not just as a head coach but as a position coach. He knew how to coach a person."

Grambling played Morgan State in the first football game at Three Rivers Stadium, and Lewis scored three touchdowns. The game didn't help him because the Steelers already knew about Lewis. They drafted the 6-foot-1, 196-pounder with a 9.4 100-yard dash time first in 1971. The Steelers also drafted Jack Ham, Gerry Mullins, Dwight White, and Larry Brown that day. On the first play of his first camp scrimmage, Lewis caught a 38-yard touchdown pass from Bob Leahy, but Lewis struggled the rest of the season with a hamstring injury and caught only three passes.

Early in the 1972 season, Lewis caught a 38-yard touchdown pass from Bradshaw with 1:08 left to beat the St. Louis Cardinals. At the time, the starter in front of Lewis, Dave Smith, was throwing his starting job away much the way he'd thrown the football away before crossing the goal line on a Monday night in Kansas City in 1971.

The season after his infamous spike, Smith complained about his contract and then defied Noll by walking to the back of the end zone instead of the sideline when Noll substituted Lewis during the sixth game of the 1972 season. Smith was traded two days later, and Lewis became the starting flanker. He finished the season with 27 catches and five touchdowns, but broke his collarbone in the regular-season finale.

Minor injuries dogged Lewis in 1973, and in 1974 he caught 30 passes, his high with the Steelers. In 1975 he injured his shoulder and caught only 17 passes. The 1976 season brought more nagging injuries and more playing time for the blossoming Stallworth as Lewis again caught 17 passes.

Lewis hit one of his patented home runs in the opening round of the 1976 playoffs. On the fourth play of the game, Bradshaw threw a 76-yard touchdown pass to Lewis. It sent Bradshaw on the way to a perfect 158.3 passer rating, not to mention a 40-14 win over the Baltimore Colts.

"Every time we ran that play in practice we scored," Lewis said. "It was a deviation from one of our basic patterns, but instead of going all the way to the corner, the slot man would fake that and break to the post. It worked every time."

The nagging injuries continued in 1977 as the Steelers acquired more young talent. Jim Smith teamed with Swann and Stallworth to make Lewis expendable, and he was traded before the 1978 season for Seymour. The Bills never compensated the Steelers for their new star, and on opening day, against the Steelers, Lewis caught a 22-yard touchdown pass. It signaled his rejuvenation.

Lewis helped the Bills become a winner under Chuck Knox before retiring over Memorial Day weekend in 1984. Lewis spent a year as an assistant coach at

Texas Southern University before he began working in his hometown as a local board director under the Workforce Investment Act. The federally funded program helps people find jobs.

"When the funding's going good and you can serve the public, those are the good days," Lewis said. "But when things aren't going so well with the funding, those are the bad days."

Even though Houma sits in the heart of the Louisiana wetlands, some 60 miles southwest of New Orleans, the area wasn't crippled by Hurricane Katrina. "We had a lot of water and wind damage," Lewis said. "But it was no comparison to what happened in other parts of the state like New Orleans. We can almost say we weren't even affected in comparison."

Lewis lives in Houma with his wife, Norma. They have a daughter, Gabrielle, and a son, Quincy. The family expected to be on hand for Lewis' induction into the Louisiana Sports Hall of Fame in the summer of 2006.

"It came as a surprise," Lewis said. "That's the last thing I was thinking about. I had a couple people in the past ask me if I would be selected to it, but it was just a passing thing. I never focused on it or thought about it."

Lewis has fond memories of Pittsburgh. Old No. 43 said that clinching the team's first division title in 1972 is his best memory.

"It was about that 40-year thing, that they hadn't won it, and when we won that division championship it was only my second year, but it was the highlight right there. That was the biggest thing that happened," he said.

What does he think about the player wearing No. 43 for the Steelers today?

"He's tough," Lewis said of Troy Polamalu. "He's a ballplayer. His effort and desire and attitude speak for itself."

Lewis had hoped for the same during his time in Pittsburgh, but a shy personality and a series of nagging injuries held him back.

"You're under the control of a lot of other things," he said. "Maybe it goes back to what Mr. Nunn said. Maybe I should've opened up a bit more, used more politics and pushed it a little more. But then again, it's a team game. I don't care how good a guy thinks he may be, without good teammates, good coaching, a good system, a lot of things won't happen, regardless of how good you are. Just like Coach Rob used to say: You're only as good as the people around you."

CHAPTER 20

Larry Brown

A reporter once asked Chuck Noll which of his former players belonged in the Hall of Fame. The first name out of Noll's mouth was Larry Brown.

"And if Chuck would've listened to us and moved him to tackle earlier," cracked scout Bill Nunn, "Larry Brown WOULD be in the Hall of Fame."

Throw on a tape of the 1979 Steelers and you'll see Brown in his prime. He was a robust pass-blocker with the quick feet to excel in Noll's trapping game. And on a line made up of 6-foot-2 players, the 6-foot-4, 275-pound Brown stood out. As Nunn said, Brown played right tackle like a Hall of Famer.

"Those are kind things and I certainly appreciate those kinds of sentiments," said Brown. "It means a lot to have people feel like that, but I'm certainly not seeking or advocating that."

Brown doesn't boast. Perhaps it's why he didn't play in his first Pro Bowl until he'd put 12 NFL seasons behind him. Others speak volumes in short sentences:

"Larry was the best offensive tackle I ever saw play the game," Tunch Ilkin said in 1984.

"If I could teach my kids to grow up to be like Larry Brown, it's the greatest thing they could do," said the late Mike Webster.

"I wish I were like him," said Mel Blount.

Great player. Great person. Renaissance man. Consider: Brown didn't use an agent to negotiate a six-figure salary with the Steelers in the early 1980s; he had considered dental school at one point, the USFL at another; he married a writer but doesn't want to discuss his family for the public record; while still playing football, he and teammate J.T. Thomas owned a couple of Burger Kings, and after Brown got out of football he and Thomas traded up to Applebee's Restaurants—13 of them.

GEORGE GOJKOVICH/GETTY IMAGES

LARRY BROWN
Seasons with Steelers: 1971-84
Position: offensive tackle
Height: 6-foot-4
Playing weight: 246 pounds

As a student at Kansas University, Brown played a new position each year. He started as a tackle, moved to linebacker, then defensive end before settling in as a senior tight end. He was drafted by the Steelers in the fifth round of the 1971 draft as a tight end and caught two passes in his first two years. In 1973, as "the blocking tight end" behind John McMakin, Brown caught five passes. In 1974, Brown caught a career-high 17 passes and became a central figure in the Super Bowl.

Against the Minnesota Vikings in Super Bowl IX, Brown became a controversial figure when, with seven minutes remaining and the Steelers nursing a 9-6 lead, he reeled in a long pass from Terry Bradshaw. Brown was hit and appeared to have fumbled, and that's what one official ruled. The ball was initially awarded to the Vikings, but another official overruled the call, calling it an incomplete pass and giving possession back to the Steelers. The Steelers continued their drive and scored with three and a half minutes left when Bradshaw threw a 1-yard bullet to Brown in the end zone for the clinching score. The ball was thrown so hard "it was buried in Brown's stomach," said assistant coach Dick Hoak.

Brown caught 16 passes for a career-high 244 yards in 1975, once again as the blocking tight end to second-year pro Randy Grossman. The Steelers drafted tight end Bennie Cunningham in the first round of the 1976 draft, but it didn't signal Brown's immediate move to tackle. Injuries played a bigger role in Brown's fate.

When Gordon Gravelle was placed on injured reserve in the middle of the 1976 season, the Steelers used Brown as a backup left tackle. He practiced at the position and played in parts of a handful of games before being moved there full-time in 1977.

"They must've liked what they saw," Brown said at the time.

"We look for a guy who can fire off the ball," said Noll. "Look at Gerry Mullins."

Mullins was another converted college tight end who'd moved to right tackle earlier in his career. Mullins settled at right guard when Brown became the right tackle in 1977. Injuries limited Brown in 1978, but he made monumental strides at the position in 1979. By the Steelers' fourth Super Bowl, the 275-pound Brown was at the peak of his ability. He was big enough and strong enough to run block, and his feet were quick enough to pass block. The combination made him a weapon for Noll.

Brown was appreciated by teammates and coaches, but not so much by the media or Pro Bowl voters. He was named a Pro Bowl alternate after the 1981 season, and finally, at the age of 33, made the Pro Bowl in 1982. He was also named to the *Football Digest*'s Most Underrated Team.

Brown considered joining fellow Steelers tackle Ray Piney in the USFL in 1983, but the upstart league wouldn't meet Brown's $1 million (over three years) asking price. He instead held out 10 days before signing with the Steelers, but his knees began to trouble him.

Brown suffered through a chronic condition in his left knee called condylar malaise. The condition limited him to eight games in 1983, but the end came in San Francisco in 1984 when Brown left the game with an injured right knee.

Brown didn't play again, but had prepared for his life's work by buying the two fast-food franchises with Thomas. After Brown retired, he and Thomas hatched their more grandiose plan.

"There were 17 other guys here in the area with Burger Kings, and it didn't seem like that was the kind of opportunity we were looking for in terms of development opportunities," Brown said. "So from that, we came across the Applebee's. That was a fairly young company with development opportunity and upside potential."

Thomas borrowed $6,000 from his mother to match Brown's $6,000, and they bought into Applebee's in 1987 and opened their first franchise in Scott Township in 1990. Through an Edgewood company named B.T. Woodlipp Inc., the two built an empire that included 13 locations by the spring of 2004. They were spread from West Virginia to State College, Pennsylvania.

Thomas was bought out in 2004 by Apple American Group of San Francisco. The group also paid down Woodlipp's debt and secured an option to acquire Brown's equity in exchange for AAG equity. Brown continues as partner and senior executive and oversees 15 locations. Thomas moved on to open a Red Hot & Blue franchise restaurant at the SouthSide Works on East Carson Street in Pittsburgh.

"It was a good move for him," Brown said. "And it's been a good situation for me. Obviously this business is quite challenging, as you might imagine, but we've been fortunate. It's been a good franchise."

When Brown looks back on the highlights of his playing days, he doesn't pick out the Super Bowl touchdown, or the two tackle-eligible touchdowns he caught from Bradshaw later in his career, or even the championships.

"I have my rings," he said. "They're large and I'll wear them if I going to see people who are interested in seeing them, but otherwise I don't. They're more like trophies than attractive pieces of jewelry, and I'm not a jewelry guy.

"I played for 14 years and it's kind of hard to go back and pick things out of that. The guys I was associated with and played with and the relationships you develop and the success I was able to be a part of, that's what I remember. I feel fortunate to have had the career I had, so I don't look back with regrets. You take what it is for what it is. I was fortunate to play and be a part of the team."

CHAPTER 21

Jack Lambert

Jack Lambert made the single *coolest* move in Steelers history when he slammed Cliff Harris to the ground for making fun of his kicker in Super Bowl X.

"Jack Lambert," Chuck Noll said after the game, "is a defender of what is right."

It's how he's lived life: Raucously just.

Not much is heard from Lambert these days. He avoids interviews ... most of the time. "My life's not going to be very exciting for you," Lambert said. "Sorry."

Lambert is a busy family man these days. He warned his rabid following as much when, at the end of a stirring and, yes, raucous Hall of Fame induction speech, Lambert asked his wife and two daughters to stand up.

"There, ladies and gentlemen," Lambert said, "is my Hall of Fame."

Since that speech in 1990, the Hall has expanded. Lambert and his wife, Lisa, have four children: Lauren, Elizabeth, John, and Ty. In 2006, 21 years since he retired, Lambert is busier than ever.

"Joe Greene called me the other night," Lambert said from the home he built just north of Pittsburgh. "We were chitting and chatting and he was telling me he has about 47 grandkids. I have four kids ages 12 to 17. I got married later in life. These guys have a lot of spare time. They can do things. Guys call me from time to time, but I tell them I'm in the situation you guys were in when we were playing. You know what I mean? It's not that I don't want to come do this stuff, it's that my wife's taking two girls to a softball game, and I've got two boys to try and get to two different games.

"There are definitely pros and cons to getting married earlier or later in life, and it's just where I'm at right now. But it's been wonderful. I enjoy so much watching the kids play. I wish I had more spare time, as far as being able to go

JACK LAMBERT
Seasons with Steelers: 1974-84
Position: middle linebacker
Height: 6-foot-4
Playing weight: 220 pounds

golfing or fishing or whatever I want to do, but in the evening it's time to run kids."

So much for the one about Jack Lambert, hermit crab. Lambert is just another busy parent in the small town of Worthington. He makes it to as many of his kids' games as mathematically possible.

"I try and stay in the background," he said. "I don't want to in any way, shape, or form take any kind of thunder away from them. Everything my kids have accomplished thus far they've done on their own, and I try and stay in the background as much as I can. I'm not yipping and yapping at coaches or anything—not that I agree with everything they do. I was never a son or daughter of a Hall of Famer, so I just try and stay out of the way for these guys and let them do their thing.

"Everything they've accomplished they've accomplished on their own, and I'm proud of them for that. They've got great grades and they're doing well in sports, and they're good kids. Their teachers seem to like them; the kids seem to like them. I think they're good kids and I'm proud of them."

Lambert had just received a call from his wife informing him that Elizabeth, a sophomore at Kittanning High School, pitched all 10 innings of a win over rival Highlands. Lambert's son John is a hockey player, which suits dad, a voracious hockey fan. Hockey leaves little time for John to play football, but 12-year-old Ty has the bug.

"I'm totally against playing football at a young age," Lambert said. "I didn't start playing football until the ninth grade. I don't think it's a good thing, I mean starting really early. In college I had teammates that played in these city leagues that started playing when they were eight and nine years old. By the time they got to college they were sick of it. And football's not like other sports. It hurts. It hurts to play. But anyway he drove me crazy last year. I wanted to put him off until this year, but he drove us crazy and we let him play last year. He seems to like it."

A chip off the old block. Lambert said his daughter Lauren might be more like him.

"My oldest is extremely intelligent. She's got great grades, so obviously she takes after me," he said.

Lauren planned to enter Allegheny College in the fall of 2006. She hoped to play both softball and basketball. In her senior season, she and Elizabeth were starters on a Kittanning basketball team that went to the WPIAL semifinals. Kittanning was beaten by future Class AAA state champion Hopewell, but after going 12-83 from 2001 to 2004 Kittanning was proud of its 19-9 season.

When Lambert's not running his children to games, or taking care of baseball fields, or tending to the home he built on 125 acres of wildlife, or escaping to fish or hunt, he'll sign autographs at card shows and make a few public appearances.

The Steelers opened two merchandise stores in Western Pennsylvania and called on Lambert each time. The fans were told not to line up more than three hours before the 2 p.m. session, but lines began forming at 8 a.m. Lambert is still the Steelers' most popular player and his autographs hold the most value. Lambert understands that value and sustains it by keeping appearances to a minimum. Show organizers note his professionalism and the care he puts into each autograph.

"My daughter's going to college next year, and I've got to pay for it," Lambert said. "My name's not Roethlisberger; my name's not Ward; my name's not Bettis. I don't lose $35,000 watches up in Detroit. I don't even know what a $35,000 watch looks like. When I lose one, I go back up to Wal-Mart and buy one that says Timex on it. It runs pretty good."

He laughs. "I don't know. I can't even relate to what these guys are doing right now."

Lambert follows the Steelers. Of the latest championship, he said: "I thought it was about time. What was it, 25 or 26 years? At my age I was starting to wonder if I was ever going to see another one again. But it was great for the city and great for the Rooneys. I'm happy for them. It's good stuff."

Lambert was the second-round pick of the Steelers in 1974. Scout Tim Rooney came back from Kent State with a story about how Lambert saved the quarterback from being kicked off the team by volunteering to run punishment laps with him. So personnel boss Art Rooney, Jr. drove up for a look. The Kent field was too muddy for practice that day, so Rooney watched Lambert dive into cinders in the parking lot to make plays.

At his first Steelers camp, Lambert replaced Henry Davis at middle linebacker and started on opening day. During the intro to one of his first Monday night games, Lambert told the nation he was from Buzzard's Breath, Wyoming. Howard Cosell bought it, and a star was born.

Lambert was the Defensive Rookie of the Year in 1974 and helped the Steelers win their first Super Bowl. Then he helped them win another. Going for three in a row in 1976, Lambert sparked the Steelers through one of the greatest stretches of defensive play in league history.

The 1-4 Steelers won their last nine games in 1976—five of them were shutouts, three in succession. In those nine games, the Steelers allowed 28 points.

Lambert was voted the NFL Defensive Player of the Year, but the Steelers were beaten in the AFC Championship game by the Oakland Raiders, 24-7.

"It was, without question, the best football team we ever had," Lambert said. "There were a lot of people that year picking Baltimore with Bert Jones, Lydell Mitchell, and those guys. They had a pretty good team, but we went up there and just crushed them [40-14]. I mean, we crushed them. But as you well know we lost Rocky and Franco. Then we went out to Oakland without Rocky and Franco and we were dead in the water.

"Somebody just asked me if I thought the Steelers could do it again next year, and I said it's awful tough to repeat. It's really tough because you're only an injury or two away from not making it. I told him about the '76 team, which was without question the best team we ever had, but we lost a couple guys and that was the end. That'll piss John Madden off because he thinks he had the best team that year, but without question we were a great team. It just goes to show you you never know what's going to happen. Look at the Steelers this year. It's a crazy game. That's why it's so much fun to watch."

Lambert made the key defensive play of the Steelers' fourth Super Bowl when he intercepted Vince Ferragamo at the Pittsburgh 14 with 5:24 left and the Steelers leading by 24-19. Lambert wasn't impressed with the win.

"People were saying how ugly the Steelers won this Super Bowl, and it was ugly. There's no question about it. But they ought to pull out the films from '79 when we played the Rams. Terry Bradshaw was the MVP of that game, and I think he threw three interceptions. He probably could've thrown two more, but they dropped them. I mean it was an ugly game. They moved the ball on us, on our defense, up and down the field. It was an ugly game but we won, and nobody really cares now if it was ugly or not. We won it. And that's all that matters with these guys. They're Super Bowl champs and God bless them. I think it's great."

Lambert agreed that the jewel of the Steelers' 2005 run was the playoff win at Indianapolis. He was asked if his Steelers had a similar jewel in their playoff wins.

"After the Raiders there were no playoff games," he said. "Those games were honest-to-God kick-ass playoff games. And after that the rest of them were something else."

Why?

"We were so similar in people: a bunch of nasty guys that liked to play. And the great thing about it, after the game Stabler would come into the locker room and we'd have a couple beers together. We hated each other on the field, but after it was over we'd say whoever wins, wins. It's good stuff, not like it is today with all the yipping and yapping and stuff that goes on. You'd just shake hands and have a beer. That's what it was about."

Lambert played four more seasons after that fourth Super Bowl. His final season was wrecked on opening day when he tore all the ligaments in his left big toe. He struggled through the season and announced his retirement in 1985.

"The first year was terrible. It was the worst," he said of retirement. "I watched every game—every second of every game. The tough thing is I played football for 20 consecutive years, and all of the sudden it was over. In a split second it's over, so that first year was really tough.

"I did a little bit of television, but you can't talk about them. You'd like to be a little bit critical, or say some things you really think, but you can't do it because those guys are still your teammates. You're only a couple months removed. It wasn't for me anyway. It was just something to do. But as each year goes by, it got a little bit easier."

Lambert was a deputy game warden for nine years, but had to give it up.

"My kids were starting to play sports, and I was in the woods on Saturdays. I said, hey, this is enough of this. I wanted to get involved with them. I managed baseball teams the last five years now, and I umpire and take care of the fields up here in Worthington, so I'm involved in a great deal of Little League. I tell you what: I really feel I had my chance to shine, and now I've got these four kids. My wife helps coach the Kittanning High School softball team. She was a volleyball player who went to Clemson on a scholarship, so we're involved with the kids' athletics and stuff."

It sounds like heaven.

"I don't know if it's heaven," he said. "I'd like to have some time where you could do your own thing. I just saw a letter lying on my desk out here that the basketball coach for next year's high school team has AAU stuff all set up for the summer. There's no break for these kids. It's not like when I was a kid. You went from one sport to another but you had your summer off. I mean, you played baseball but you had some time off. These kids now, it's just year around. They don't stop.

"I don't know. It just seems to me that kids need time to be kids, too. They need to go out and go fishing, walk in the woods, have some time to themselves. All this regimented stuff constantly, I don't know. But this is 2006, right? And I guess this is the way things are."

CHAPTER 22

Donnie Shell

Donnie Shell, he of the NFL-record interception total, four Super Bowl rings, and spot on the Steelers' all-time team, likes what he sees of Troy Polamalu, the guy playing his former position.

"He's the real deal," said the man who knows a real deal when he sees one.

Shell is one of the top front-office men in the NFL, the real deal of the Personnel Development set. It's a new position, as far as front-office jobs go, but it's a position that was needed and Shell was the perfect trailblazer.

"We've had one of the best programs in the NFL," he said, and the trophy case backs him up: The Carolina Panthers' director of player development won the NFL's "Best Player Programs" awards in 1998 and 1999 and the "Most Outstanding Player Programs" honor in the NFC in 2000. In 2002, the NFL just named the award after him—the Winston/Shell Award.

Shell entered the field in 1994. He was selling real estate in Columbia, South Carolina, when one of his business partners invited him to a meeting with an old classmate, Mark Richardson, who was in town pitching the PSL concept of buying season tickets for the expansion Panthers.

Richardson, the current president, and then-president Mike McCormack visited Shell's office and invited him to the presentation that evening.

"He asked me why I stayed for the whole meeting," Shell said. "I told him that if he's trying to get a National Football League team into Carolina, I would definitely be interested, because I was born and raised here."

Shell was granted an interview and was hired in 1994. He coordinates all programs for the players and their families. The core programs are continued education, financial education, and career internships. Shell earned a master's degree in counseling and guidance at South Carolina State during his playing days with the Steelers. It helps in his current position, but it doesn't cover all of his duties.

"I'm a counselor, a coach, and a mentor," he said. "We're behind the scenes working to assist the players and their families to be successful while they're here, and also when they transition from the game."

Some of the program's success stories: Dwight Stone, the former Steeler, is now a Charlotte police officer; Kevin Donnalley, who went through the high school coaches internship program, is now a head coach in Charlotte; and Mike Rucker, who went through seven internships, started Vision Group Realty for commercial and residential real estate, and the Ruckus House—a child-care facility.

"We've also had people go through and complete their degrees," Shell said.

With his pattern of success, it's a wonder Shell doesn't rise to the top of the Panthers' organization.

"I'm as high as I can go in player development. I've been the director since '94," he said. "I like what I'm doing. You've got to know your calling."

When Shell was a young man, his calling was to knock heads and intercept passes for the Steelers. He was passed over in the 1974 NFL draft, but surfaced with the Steelers as a rookie free agent. Shell believes a blood clot in his thigh, which forced him to miss the first half of the Orange Blossom Classic, cost him a chance to be drafted.

Scout Bill Nunn made sure Shell and his college coach knew the Steelers were interested, and Shell passed up better offers from Denver and Houston because of Nunn. With the Steelers, Shell was part of a terrific crop of rookie talent, and those rookies were aided by an NFL players strike that summer.

On the first day of 1974 training camp, 41 rookies crossed a "picket line" manned by several good-natured—even beer-drinking—veterans who were stationed on a back road at St. Vincent College. They stood behind a cornfield and the cemetery and did not block access to practice. By the first preseason game, eight veterans reported. Among them were quarterback Joe Gilliam and defensive tackle Ernie Holmes, and they were the leaders of a rookie lineup that dismantled the New Orleans Saints, 26-7. Shell, the former linebacker at S.C. State, started at cornerback for the Steelers.

The next week the Steelers bombed the Chicago Bears, 50-21, and reporters began calling the crop of rookies Noll's best ever. Little did they know the crop would become the best in NFL history. The strike broke and the veterans reported for the third preseason game, but a record 14 rookies made the team. The group was headed by future Hall of Famers Lynn Swann, Jack Lambert, John Stallworth and Mike Webster. Shell and another free agent, tight

DONNIE SHELL
Seasons with Steelers: 1974-87
Position: strong safety
Height: 5-foot-11
Playing weight: 190 pounds

end Randy Grossman, also became part of a group of 22 players who would win four Super Bowls.

On the first day of practice with the vets, Shell knocked receiver Ron Shanklin over with a chuck during a light passing drill. It drew a rebuke from Chuck Noll, but Shell didn't back down.

"I want to tackle a pro running back just to see what it's like," he said after that practice. "I want to hit Franco Harris. I want to hit them all."

Shell got his chance a few days later when he and Rocky Bleier collided, but Shell hit the ground and Bleier continued running.

"Did you think you were running into one of those wide receivers?" Dick Hoak shouted across the practice field. It was a good-natured catcall to a player who would one day take down the biggest and the baddest running backs the league had to offer.

The Steelers used Shell at safety and cornerback in the third exhibition game, and he knocked 6-foot-8 wide receiver Harold Carmichael out of the game. Shell also starred on special teams that game, and that's where the 190-pounder made his mark in 1974. The Steelers won the Super Bowl that season and Shell used his $25,000 winnings to buy his mother a house and donate to the South Carolina State scholarship fund. He said that his mother deserved it for raising him and his nine siblings while dad worked in the cotton mills. He said that without his school, he'd "probably be in the welfare lines."

Shell opened the 1975 season on special teams again, but pulled off a unique feat in the opener when he caught a pass on a fake punt and later intercepted a pass. The 19-yard reception was topped later in the season by Shell's 20-yard reception from punter Bobby Walden.

The Steelers won their second Super Bowl that season, and at the next camp Shell was named the team's first special-teams captain. He surrendered the job the next summer for fear of being typecast as a special-teams player only.

He wasn't. In 1977 Shell moved into the starting lineup because of injuries and led the defensive backs in tackles. The next year, with Glen Edwards gone, Mike Wagner moved to free safety and Shell became the full-time starting strong safety. He didn't come out of the position until he retired with his good friend Stallworth after the 1987 season.

In 14 seasons, Shell played in more games (201) than any Steeler but Webster (220). Shell intercepted 51 passes, the most by any strong safety in league history. He was named to five consecutive Pro Bowls (1978-82) and his torpedo hit on rookie Earl Campbell late in the 1978 season remains one of the most spectacular tackles in league history. Shell was named team MVP in 1980 and played what he felt was his best game in Cleveland in 1981, when he intercepted Browns quarterback Brian Sipe three times.

Shell was a Pro Football Hall of Fame finalist in 2001, but didn't get in. He's a member of the College Football Hall of Fame, as well as the Hall of Fame at South Carolina State, where he also played center field on the baseball team. The Charlotte Touchdown Club recognizes its high school defensive player of the year with the Donnie Shell Award. He has three children and a wife, Paulette, to whom he's been married 30 years.

What stands out when Shell reflects on his days with the Steelers?

"The Rooneys, first of all," he said. "They're business people and very good family-oriented people and community minded. Also, Coach Noll and his influence as a coach and mentor to us, the things he taught us. And the camaraderie that we had among our teammates that still exists today. Those are the three significant things."

What did Noll teach him?

"He not only taught us how to play football, he taught us how to be a professional. I remember he always asked us what we did in the summer. My first two years in the league I went back and completed my master's degree, and I remember we were doing some drills and he came over and leaned over. I thought it was another player or another coach and he said, 'I heard you completed your master's degree. Congratulations.' He always encouraged us to be the best we could be on and off the football field, whether it was reading a book to get better or talking to somebody."

Shell came close to winning his fifth ring in 2003, but the New England Patriots doused the Panthers' hopes with a last-second field goal. Shell was beaten to that fifth ring by Joe Greene two years later.

"I'll congratulate him at Mel Blount's fundraiser up there next month," Shell said. "I think it's great. They put together a great string and had a great run at it."

CHAPTER 23

Dwayne Woodruff

Chuck Noll retired at the end of the 1991 season, but the Steel Curtain era ended on the first day of training camp in 1991. That's when Dwayne Woodruff retired. He was the last remaining player from the 1970s Super Bowl teams.

The end of one era meant the beginning of another for Woodruff, who became Judge Woodruff in 2005. He was appointed and elected to the Allegheny County Common Pleas Court, juvenile section, and began serving just before Christmas.

"I'm now in a position to continue to work with kids and try to help kids," he said from his chambers. "Service is extremely big in my household. To have a job like this, too, is the best of both worlds for me."

Woodruff began this era during the previous one. He began studies at Duquesne Law School during the 1984 season. He studied football six days and law five nights in what became a four-year struggle to maximize every minute of every day.

"I wouldn't recommend it for anybody," his wife Joy told the *Pittsburgh Press* after it was all over. "It was a bit much."

The father of three small children, Woodruff's most difficult year was his third of law school. He tore two ligaments and some cartilage in his knee during the third preseason game of 1986 and had to sit out the season. His mother died of cancer two weeks after the injury. Woodruff used her battle as inspiration to not only recover from his injury but to finish school. And since he wasn't playing, there would be more time.

Or would there?

"It's not any easier," Woodruff said at the time. "If anything it's more difficult getting to class on crutches and staying out of everybody's way."

The Steelers finished 1986 with their worst record (6-10) since 1970. Without Woodruff the secondary was a mess, so the Steelers drafted Rod

DWAYNE WOODRUFF
Seasons with Steelers: 1979-85; 1987-90
Position: cornerback
Height: 5-foot-11
Playing weight: 198 pounds

Woodson, Delton Hall, and Thomas Everett in the first four rounds of the 1987 draft. Woodruff recovered in time to hold his job at left cornerback. He even earned a new three-year contract. He graduated from law school with a 3.2 grade average in May of 1988 and the resumption of basic family living was on.

"I don't remember a whole lot about that time," he said almost 18 years later. "At that point my life was so structured, time-wise, because I was trying to get everything in in a day. It's almost like you're not living yourself. You're just going day to day just trying to get things done."

In spite of the impressive young cornerbacks on the team, Woodruff held his football job until 1990, when D.J. Johnson replaced him. Woodruff turned down a Steelers offer in 1991 and announced his retirement at St. Vincent College. At the time he ranked third among active AFC players with 37 interceptions. The total ranked him fourth in Steelers history at the time.

Woodruff started working for the law firm Meyer Darragh during his latter playing days. He stayed there nine years before forming his own law firm: Woodruff, Flaherty & Fardo. His experience as a trial attorney involved civil, tax, and family cases. He announced his intention to become a judge on the Common Pleas Court in late 2004 and a year later was on the bench.

"I've had four jobs, and I'm still in the same three- or four-block area," he said. "I stayed in the same garage the whole time."

Woodruff won his primary, was appointed by the governor and then won the election in November. But why the appointment?

"There were a couple reasons," he said. "One, the voters had already spoken in the primary. I was the leading vote-getter in the primary, and also what I thought—he didn't say this to me—but a number of the senators also felt that Allegheny County needed to have more diversity on the bench. I think they wanted to have a black male because we have a good number of young black men that come through here. To balance and restore the justice, you ought to have a black male figure here. That is extremely important in a number of ways: Not just in regard to law, but also in regard to perception and how the kids that come through here will see the court."

In a brief time, Woodruff came to understand the emotional roller coaster that comes with the job.

"Emotionally I go from top to bottom every day with these kids," he said. "You see some great things, how they turn their lives around, and then you see how devastating some of their lives have been and the choices that they make, the lack of guidance and support in their homes. It just tears you apart. You do that on a daily basis. To me, it can be difficult at times."

Is he a tough judge? Woodruff chuckled at the question. "Well, I'm tough on a number of things," he said. "One, I believe kids should go to school every day. In 90 percent of my orders, there's an order in there for them to go to school every day, and it's strictly enforced. Regardless of what they're doing, if they don't get their education, it's just going to get worse down the line. That's important. I'm very tough on guns as well. That's another issue.

"But outside of that, we just try to find a program or something that's going to help these young men and women turn their lives around and have an opportunity to be successful, to go out and make a difference in society. A lot of these kids just don't feel that they have a chance at all in life. They've never been supported; they've never been loved; they've never been directed the right way, just in simple things: How do you act when you go out to dinner in public? How do you walk? If you're at a meeting, how do you conduct yourself? They have no idea. They just haven't been taught some basic things you need to know in life just to get along."

Woodruff had just returned from a trip to Erie with several other judges to visit the programs to which they send juvenile offenders. Woodruff came back hopeful.

"It's amazing how they've turned around and how they feel about themselves, the self-esteem they have that they didn't have at all," he said. "But when you talk to some of them, they don't want to go back home. That's sad. Even though they're turning their lives around and learning and soaking all this stuff in, the situation, what they've gone through in their lives, is sad."

Woodruff and his wife practice and preach community involvement at home. Their oldest daughter, Jillian, graduated from Duke and was in her first year of residency as an Ob/Gyn at Cornell Hospital in New York. Daughter Jenyce graduated from American University, where she studied law and basketball. As a senior she finished third in the conference in rebounding. She's now at Duquesne Law School after working for her father's firm since she was a sophomore in high school. Son John entered his second year at West Virginia University in 2006 and was looking forward to his first season as a defensive back on the football team after sitting out 2005 with a redshirt.

"We've got good kids," Woodruff said. "You've got to get on them every now and then, but overall they work hard and they all have a heart for community service as well, which is great. I'm very proud of all three of our kids."

Woodruff's No. 10 is retired at the University of Louisville, right next to the retired No. 16 of John Unitas. Woodruff was drafted in the sixth round by the Steelers in 1979 and became a valuable nickel back for the Super Bowl champions that season. Woodruff went on to lead the team in interceptions five times and was voted team MVP in 1982 after intercepting five passes in the strike-shortened season. That was enough to tie him for the league lead with Donnie Shell, Bobby Jackson, and Ken Riley.

"The thing I remember most about playing is just the guys," Woodruff said. "It's just like work now. I just love coming to work. I tell my kids, whatever you do, make sure you love doing it. I loved going to work every day and practicing and just hanging out with the guys. It was extremely satisfying. I loved that part.

"Obviously the Super Bowl was a beautiful thing, going through that and seeing how the town got all excited and got behind the Steelers. That's one of the reasons we made our home here. The people just welcomed me and my family with open arms from day one, which was wonderful. They don't do that with everybody, but we were fortunate to be taken in by the area. Of course, playing the game itself was a lot of fun, particularly since I was fortunate to be on a number of winning teams. It always seemed more fun when you were winning."

Does Woodruff plan to follow in Byron "Whizzer" White's footsteps and go from the Pittsburgh Steelers to the United State Supreme Court?

"I'm happy where I am," he said. "I think the Lord's going to do some different things for me and the kids while I'm here. I'm anxiously looking to see what that's going to be."

CHAPTER 24

Tunch Ilkin
& Craig Wolfley

Tunch Ilkin and Craig Wolfley played on the same offensive line throughout the 1980s before becoming part of the Pittsburgh sports media late in the 1990s. Until August of 2006, they hosted a morning talk show on Fox Sports 970 called *In The Locker Room*. It sounded something like this:

"I come to this country to play American football from Istanbul, Turkey," Ilkin said in a brief flurry of native dialect. "I immigrated to the States and my father's name was Mehmet and my mother's name is Ayten, and it was a typical immigrant family. We came to America, the land of opportunity, and I grew up in the Chicago area. I went to Indiana State in Terre Haute, Indiana, because it was the only college to offer me a scholarship. It was a great place to go to college.

"I met my wife of 24 years there and got drafted by the Steelers in the sixth round. My mom thought I got drafted into the army. That was kind of tough. I had to calm her down. She freaked because I wasn't home, and Chuck called my house in Chicago. My mom answered and she freaked out. True story. We're talking 1980 and the Vietnam war had been done for a while, but my mom thought there was still a draft."

"I'm from Buffalo, New York," Wolfley said in a miffed tone. "I went to Syracuse University. I came out in 1980. There, how was that? Gee thanks, for letting me have a little tape."

The two broke into laughter. They know each other so well they can see the jokes coming but are still amused.

"Tell him more," said Tunch. "You went to the big school."

"The only difference is I flew to games," Wolf said. "He came from the bus league. Anyway, my 15-year-old sister answered the phone on draft day, and she was talking away for several minutes. I figured it was my grandma because she liked to call every 10 minutes to ask if I got drafted. Finally that call came in, and I was heading out the door because it was after the draft had supposedly shut down, and so my sister stopped talking and said, 'Hey, it's for you.' I asked her who it was and she said, 'I don't know, some guy from Pittsburgh named Chuck.' She'd been talking to Chuck Noll for three minutes. How somebody like Chuck had a conversation with my turkey sister for three minutes is beyond me, but he pulled it off."

The two players were drafted in 1980, three months after the Steelers won their fourth Super Bowl. The roster was stacked; the fans rabid.

"I was shocked I got drafted," Tunch said. "I was not supposed to be drafted. My agent told me I would either be a late-round pick or a free agent, so it was a real shock. The irony for me was that at Indiana State probably 40 percent of our team was from western Pennsylvania, so I had Steeler fans all around me all the time, and being that I'd grown up in Chicago and was a big Bear fan, I hated the Steelers, so all my buddies were busting my chops, going: 'What are you going to do? Tell Chuck you don't want to go?' They knew I hated the Steelers, but it was a great celebration, and then reality set in, that I was going to the four-time Super Bowl champions, and I wondered how I was going to make this team.

"The first day of training camp, there were like 18,000 fans at St. Vincent College. It was packed with people. We didn't get that kind of crowd for homecoming at Indiana State. It was unbelievable, and then I'm looking at all these Hall of Famers, and I didn't know if I should be on the practice field with them or get their autographs because I was thinking that if I got cut I didn't want to go home empty-handed."

Wolf: "Back then they brought the rookies in a week early, so we'd already gone through a week of training camp. At lunch we watched Jon Kolb, John Stallworth, Lynn Swann, Mike Webster, Joe Greene, one after another. These great players were walking through, and you just didn't know what to do. Do you say Mr. Greene or hi Joe? How do you do this? They were that impressive. I'll never forget it."

Ilkin became a two-time Pro Bowler, and fans voted Wolfley to the Steelers' all-time team. They were asked to describe the action in the trenches.

"It's like an alley fight," Tunch said. "It's a battle. It's very intense, anything goes, anything that you don't get flagged for, and everybody's fighting for every inch of territory you can, whether you're run-blocking or pass-blocking. It's a team thing, a team concept, us five offensive linemen against the defense, but then again it's a man-on-man thing. It's me against the guy across from me. The team concept of it makes you not want to lose your battle because it affects the

OTTO GREULE JR./GETTY IMAGES

TUNCH ILKIN
Seasons with Steelers: 1980-92
Position: offensive tackle
Height: 6-foot-3
Playing weight: 263 pounds

whole thing, and then the pride concept of me against you, man on man, makes you want to win that battle all that more. It's something. It's like an alley fight; controlled rage."

Wolf: "It's kind of funny because you go into a game and the parameters are very loose. There's no hard and fast set of rules, more like general guidelines of conduct in there, and it really comes down to you and the other guy and just how bitter does it get that day, because you don't know. There are times when you play very cleanly, but if somebody starts something it can be every other play you're down on the ground and you are punching, kneeing, rolling up, doing anything you can to aggravate, agitate, honk off, tick off, anything you can do to get under the skin of one of the guys in the other jersey. Do you remember the linebacker from Detroit?"

Tunch: "Chris Spielman?"

Wolf: "Oh, yeah, Chris Spielman. Before a game, Kenny Dallafior, a good buddy of ours who used to play with us but was with Detroit, he went up to Chris Spielman and said that he used to play with the Steelers and that Tunch and Wolf were talking about you, that you weren't really a tough guy and that you don't bring it, that you stink. He was joking around but he forgets to tell Spielman before the game that he was just joking. So during the game, every other time I lock up with Spielman we get in this pushing-punching match and he's saying, 'What do you think of me now? Am I a tough guy now? Do I stink now?' After the game I went up to Dallafior and asked him what's the problem with Spielman. He said, 'Oh, uh, I was kidding around before the game and told him you guys thought he sucked. I forgot to tell him I was only joking.' I said great. Thanks."

Tunch: "There's a lot of that going on, a lot of talking going on. There are always guys that you don't like and there are battles. For me the biggest battle was always with Ray Childress. I used to go against him twice a year, and we flat-out didn't like each other."

Wolf: "But you were the king of the premeditated aggravation, too. You'd tell me going into games, 'Watch this first play.' And I'd tell you I'm a little busy, but give me a report after. Like Al Noga from Minnesota. He was a high-strung, high-wired athlete, and Tunch said, 'I'm going to honk him off. I'm going to punch him right in the face to set the tone.' Sure enough he'd do it, and on the second play I'd hear Noga saying, 'Hey, Ilkin, I'm not afraid of you.' I'd think, oh, he did it."

Tunch: "We used to cover each other's back. We were down in Houston one year and we only had one quarterback, Mark Malone. Bradshaw was hurt and Stoudt was hurt. So Malone scores a touchdown on a run play, and Vernon Perry, a safety for the Oilers, comes up and clearly—a good second after he scored the touchdown—spears him when he goes down. Vernon Perry does a somersault on his knees, and I'm trailing the play and I come up and I just unload on Vernon Perry while he's on his knees, and I roll over him. Ted Washington Sr. jumps on my back. Wolf jumps on Ted Washington's back and grabs him by the facemask and starts pummeling him. And then somebody jumps on Wolf's back, and I jump on this guy. It was a brawl in the end zone, and it was just us two against them, last game of the season. They break it up, and Vernon Perry says to me, 'I'm going to get you after the game, Ilkin. I'm

GEORGE GOJKOVICH/GETTY IMAGES

CRAIG WOLFLEY
Seasons with Steelers: 1980-89
Position: offensive guard
Height: 6-foot-1
Playing weight: 265 pounds

going to come and kill you after the game.' That just does it for me. I'm just gone. I don't even remember what I started screaming."

Wolf: "And so at the end of the game we're standing on the sidelines at the 50-yard line. He's looking like he's going to sprint, and we're watching the clock count down and he goes, 'Watch my back. I'm going for Perry.' Sure enough at the gun he takes off for the Oiler bench and Vernon Perry was already heading off to the end zone. I'm trying to keep up, and I thought that maybe it wasn't such a good idea for the two of us taking off like this. What were we going to do? We didn't even have an Alamo for crying out loud."

Tunch: "And in our day you played the same guy year in and year out. In the division you played him twice a year, so the animosity could build."

Do players reconcile, or repair, these relationships?

Tunch: "Ray Childress and I were at the Pro Bowl together, and he was a good guy. Some guys you never end up liking."

Wolf: "I met Randy White off the field, and it was the first civil conversation we ever had. That was a very bitter one because he was an intense player, and so was I. It came to pugilism a couple of times, but he's a great guy. You kind of bury those old indiscretions."

Do you laugh this much on the field?

Tunch: "Yeah. One of the funniest stories for me was when we were playing the Browns and they came with an all-out blitz, and Malone gets jacked from both sides; I mean knocked out. His helmet flies up in the air, hits the ground, both ear pads come out of the helmet, and he's lying on the ground, out. His helmet's next to him, both ear pads are on the ground, and there's me, Wolf, and Webby and not one of us goes to help him up, and we all do the same thing: 'I got my guy; it wasn't my guy that killed him.'"

Wolf: "It's cover your own butt. I remember that so vividly because I'm standing there and Webby and I are arguing with Bobby Golic, the nose tackle, on whether he came backside or not, which would've changed the blitz pattern and the pickups. I said, 'Bob, you came backside, right?' He's looking at me, looking at Webby, and he didn't know who he should agree with. But we're interrogating the guy while Mark's eyes are rolled up and blood's coming out of his mouth. Then there was Detroit when we lost 45-3 on Thanksgiving Day, the Thanksgiving Day slaughter back in the early '80s. We were already down like 35-0 in the third quarter, and they replaced our quarterback, Stoudter, with Malone. And Malone came in during a timeout and he starts giving this rah-rah, prep-school speech, that 'We can do this' stuff. But nothing has worked all day long, alright.

"The game started, and then it was over within 90 seconds. It was just an avalanche of Detroit scoring plays that hit us. It's one of those days where nothing works, and he's in there giving us this rah-rah stuff. I'll never forget when Mike Webster just looked at him—and Mike could do a great Bill Murray—and Mark goes, 'We can do this,' and Webby looked at him and in his best Bill Murray said, 'There's no way in hell we can do this.' The three of us started laughing, and it was hard to stop. We had to peek to see if Chuck saw us on the sideline, because we're laughing in the huddle when we're down 35-0. And what was the year we almost set a record for the most blocked punts?"

Tunch: "That was 1988, the year when we were in Cleveland and Webby snapped three into Lake Erie. It was funny because, you know, Webby was our hero, and he was snapping them high all day long. He'd come in and he'd be like three feet over Newsome's head."

Wolf: "Three feet? How about 30 feet?"

Tunch: "And he'd come in and ask us if that one was too high, and we'd go, oh, no, he should've had it."

Wolf: "After the second time, we were on the verge of setting an NFL record for the most blocked punts, and he sails it and we had to hide because it was to the point of absolute hilarity. It's so pressure-packed that sometimes you get almost the exact opposite response than what you would think."

Tunch: "I remember we were playing Cincinnati, and they were running that 46 Bears defense. It was the first year teams were running it, and we had this base protection against it. We'd take the three inside guys and the middle linebacker and turn to the outside linebacker. Cincinnati took Emanuel King, who was like an outside linebacker but the size of a defensive end, and they had him outside the tight end, which meant that Walter Abercrombie had to pick him up on a blitz. They were running that play, and Abercrombie was getting mulched by Emanuel King. We came off the field after Malone got drilled like three times, and Chuck came screaming at me, 'You can't do that! You can't do that! You can't do that!' I said what are you talking about? He said, 'Emanuel King is killing Walter!' I said Chuck, it's 46, it's base turn. He said, 'You can't do that!' I said Chuck, it's 46, base turn, so either change our rules or change the play. He said, 'OK, just do it!' And he walks away, and I didn't know whether we were changing the play or changing the rules."

Wolf: "I was standing next to him, and I wasn't going to ask him."

Tunch: "So we didn't know what to do. We had this heated screaming match, and after he walks away, I said, well, what do we do? Then we just called our own stuff."

Wolf: "Remember Miami? The first play with John Offerdahl, the inside linebacker from the Dolphins, he does a finger poke, crushes me in the eye. I got hit so bad on the first play down in Miami, there was blood all over my hand and I couldn't see out of my eye. It felt like my eyeball had moved."

Tunch: "He thought his eyeball was bleeding. 'My eye's bleeding!'"

Wolf: "So I go, 'Webby, check my eye.' I'm like Popeye. I'm looking at him with one eye, and I asked him if my eye was still there. It hurt so bad. I got hit so hard. Webby got beat on the first play, and he don't even want to look. He said, 'I don't know. I've got bigger problems.' I said, 'You can't even look to see if my eye's still in the socket?' He said, 'I've got to get ready for the next play.' I'm thinking my eyeball's hanging out, and he ain't got the minute to tell me if the thing is hanging out or not."

Tunch: "'My eye's bleeding! My eye's bleeding!' I said, it ain't your eye; it's your eyebrow. There's no sympathy amongst buddies in there. I tell you, there's none. I come back in the huddle and my finger's dislocated. It's sticking out and I said, ow, would somebody pull it? And everyone goes, 'Oooh.' I couldn't get anybody to pull my finger back. Anything that's sticking out the wrong way, nobody wants anything to do with it."

Wolf: "I told him I already know that joke. Pull the finger and you cut one."

Tunch: "That's what he said. I ask Webby and he said, 'Get that thing away from me.'"

Wolf: "What about your second year when you developed that nervous stomach?"

Tunch: "Oh, my."

Wolf: "Tunch develops this problem with projectile vomiting, and about halfway through practice, when he was heated up and we were in the heavy part of it, he gets sick. And I mean, he just let a geyser go. It looked like *The Exorcist*, he puked so hard.

"So we're in Cleveland for a preseason game, and in the second half Tunch is in there playing center. He comes out, and I can hear him as we're coming to the line of scrimmage. He's making this growling noise. His stomach is getting upset, and I'm playing left guard right next to him. Ron Simmons is the nose tackle, a big Florida State kid playing across from him. Now, Stoudter's the quarterback, and he comes up to the line and he's looking over the defense. I hear Tunch start to growl and grumble. He's holding it down, and into the count Stoudter goes, and I see Tunch shudder. All of the sudden, one heartbeat before the snap of the ball, he lets go and pukes right in the face of Ron Simmons. He hit him right in the facemask. And we're double-teaming him. We fire out on him and he can't see.

"We go back to the huddle and I asked him if he's OK. Now I'm standing right next to him in the huddle, and he turns and yaks right on my foot. I said what did you do that for? Why didn't you turn the other way? So now I move about three feet away from Tunch. We have this circle in the huddle and then there's a gap of three feet between Tunch and me. So we go up to the line of scrimmage and Ron Simmons is there swearing his head off at Tunch. He now begins to play the nose tackle position that Golic later made famous, where he'd get three yards off the line of scrimmage. Golic played it purposefully; Simmons didn't want Tunch to puke on him again. So we come to the sideline and Rollie Dotsch says, 'What is going on in the huddle?' I said what do you mean? He said, 'Why are you standing three feet from Tunch? We don't want the defensive guys to see the quarterback's mouth in case they can read lips.' I said, he's throwing up on me, Rollie. What do you want me to do? I said look at the yak all over my foot."

The Steelers made the playoffs only one time in the second half of the 1980s. How did Noll handle it?

Wolf: "He never changed."

Tunch: "Yeah, he was always the same. He was always the teacher, always working to get better. He never panicked. Even after we lost those two games 51-0 and 41-10 to start 1989, his line was, 'I hope we just played the two best teams in the National Football League.' And he called us in and he was really worried about the way we were processing information, because the media was saying the game had passed Chuck by and we were a terrible football team. When he met with us on Wednesday that week he said, 'Be careful what you allow into your brain, because your brain is like a swimming pool.' And he went through the chemical breakdown of the swimming pool. I think he sensed he was losing us in the meeting, so he said, 'In other words, don't let anybody piss in your pool!' I think it worked, because we ended up having a real good season."

Wolf: "It was his steadiness that made that season. That was a team that easily could've slid off the edge of the precipice. Any other coach would've lost that team."

Tunch: "And that was our rallying cry: Don't let anybody piss in your pool."

CHAPTER 25

Louis Lipps

Defensive coordinator Tony Dungy never saw better quickness off the line. Offensive coordinator Tom Moore compared the rookie's jumping ability to Lynn Swann's. Further proof that Louis Lipps was a certified threat could be found in John Stallworth's 1984 statistics. Stallworth had career highs in receptions (80), receiving yards (1,395), and touchdown catches (11) that year, and he was catching the passes from Mark Malone and David Woodley, not Terry Bradshaw.

Lipps, the 1984 NFL Rookie of the year, opened up the field like no Steelers receiver had since Swann was in his prime. Lipps caught 45 passes as a rookie and led the AFC by averaging 19.1 yards per catch.

He didn't wait long to prove he could play. In the opener against Kansas City Lipps caught six passes for 183 yards and two touchdowns. The first of those touchdowns was an 80-yard catch and run past veteran safety Deron Cherry.

"All I wanted to do was spike the football," Lipps remembered. "I spiked the ball so hard I must've chased it 30 yards in the end zone just so I could keep it as a souvenir. Bennie Cunningham was the one who actually told me to go and grab the ball: 'It's your first one. You've got to keep the ball.' And so I had to chase this ball down after spiking it so hard, because that's the one thing I wanted to do when I got to the end zone, and I spiked it pretty good."

The veterans gave him another ball, the game ball, afterward, and he was named the AFC Player of the Week. And after three games, Lipps had 15 catches for 337 yards and four touchdowns. He was a new sensation and he made it seem so easy.

He could also return punts. As a rookie, Lipps compiled 656 return yards, which still stands as an NFL rookie record. Even though he had returns of 54 and 76 yards nullified by penalties, no one has approached the record since.

LOUIS LIPPS
Seasons with Steelers: 1984-91
Position: wide receiver
Height: 5-foot-10
Playing weight: 190 pounds

Lipps made the Pro Bowl in 1984 as a punt returner, the first Steelers rookie to make it since Franco Harris in 1972. Lipps returned to the Pro Bowl in 1985 as a receiver after catching 59 passes for 1,134 yards and 12 touchdowns. He scored 15 touchdowns overall, which remains a Steelers record, and he was voted the team's MVP. Those 1985 numbers were career highs for a player who caught over 50 passes each season from 1988 to 1991.

"My first few years were just a blast," Lipps said from his office in Pittsburgh. "I was Rookie of the Year, went to the Pro Bowl. Those things in itself were just so overwhelming for me. And then the next year all I heard from the reporters from all over was the sophomore jinx kind of thing, and I made it into something I wasn't going to think about. I put it in the back of my mind and just tried to have the same kind of year I did my first year, and I did. I had a better year and went back to the Pro Bowl, and it just kind of went from there. In the latter part of the '80s we kind of sputtered a little bit, although we did make the playoffs within that stint. And also, my rookie year we did make the playoffs, we won the Central division, we went all the way to the championship game, one game from the Super Bowl, but we didn't make it. To do all that in my rookie year was just a great achievement for me."

The Steelers beat the host Denver Broncos, 24-17, in the 1984 playoffs, but lost to the Miami Dolphins and second-year quarterback Dan Marino in the AFC Championship game. The Dolphins lost in the Super Bowl, and Marino never made it back. Lipps never made it.

"When you're a rookie, and you make it to the championship your first year, the next year the only thing on your mind is winning one more game to go to the Super Bowl," Lipps said. "Well, I came to find out it's not that easy. You definitely have to play each and every week like it's your last game if you want to go to the Super Bowl."

Lipps is remembered for being Looed every time he dropped back to return a punt. The quarterbacks were booed; Lipps was "looed."

"I was facing the big gondola when they first did it," he said of the Three Rivers Stadium scoreboard. "They just had this huge L with all these O's behind it. That's how I knew right off that's what they were saying. The people watching on TV didn't understand why they were booing this kid who was having a pretty good game until the commentators explained. It just sent such a chill through your body that you just didn't want to sit there and catch the ball, you wanted to catch the ball and do something with it. And I tried to do that every chance I got."

Lipps learned the art of punt returning from Coach Jim Carmody at Southern Mississippi.

"Special teams held a special spot in his heart," Lipps said. "When we'd begin practice with our special teams, catching punts, he'd have people running and tugging on you while you tried to catch the ball, or he'd get people two inches from your face while you were trying to catch the ball just to keep your concentration on the ball. He's the one that kind of taught me how to locate the football as if you were an outfielder playing baseball. You line yourself up with the ball and took a peek at the baserunner to see if he's going to take off so you could set yourself up for the throw. It was the same thing with the returns."

Lipps was ranked fifth on the overall draft board by the Steelers and they were able to select him with the 23rd pick. He signed early with the Steelers and led the team in receptions in the preseason, so Noll played him right away ahead of veterans Gregg Garrity and Wayne Capers. Lipps came in time to rejuvenate Stallworth, and the two started at wide receiver for four seasons.

"Stallworth was definitely the father of the group. Everybody looked up to him," Lipps said. "He would always give you tidbits on how to recognize different coverages or how to change up your route releases to confuse defensive backs. So as far as that was concerned, man, he was another coach on the field for us. This guy played with so much confidence and competitiveness that it couldn't do anything but rub off on you."

Hamstring problems bothered Lipps throughout a large portion of his career. He injured his left hamstring in the 1986 training camp and was nagged that season by toe, back and (right) hamstring injuries. He also sustained a concussion off the elbow of Chicago's Otis Wilson while attempting to throw a block. Charges and counter-charges were followed by letters of apology and acceptance by the two principals, and Lipps returned the following Sunday—while Wilson was suspended—and caught eight passes for 150 yards and two touchdowns in a win over Detroit.

Lipps caught only 38 passes in 1986, and then only 11 in 1987. After the 24-day players' strike that season, Lipps pulled his troublesome hamstring on the first day back.

Lipps came back strong in 1988. Teamed with new quarterback Bubby Brister, Lipps caught 205 passes the next four years, but the two players were banished by new Coach Bill Cowher in 1992. Brister was benched in favor of Neil O'Donnell, and Lipps was waived after a lengthy holdout. Lipps signed with the New Orleans Saints early in the 1992 season, but re-injured his troublesome hamstring and was let go. He re-signed with the Steelers, but tore the hamstring for good in a 1993 preseason game.

Lipps has worked for Steel City Mortgage Services as a marketing manager and banking officer since 2000. Lipps also dabbles in the media. He works the KDKA Sunday pregame radio shows and is a regular member of The Chat Pack talk show from Mountaineer Park. It's a job he never considered during his playing days.

"Oh no, heck no," he said. "We were always trying to dodge you guys, man. But I like it. I really like it. The guys I work with don't make it seem like work. We have a lot of fun with it."

Lipps returned to his home in Reserve, Louisiana, to enter the construction business with his cousin in 1995. He returned to Pittsburgh in 1999.

"It was like I was only gone for a weekend. It was just an amazing feeling," he said. "These people just don't forget. They really don't forget. This has always been and always will be a sports town, and if they like you, well, they're going to like you for eternity."

RICK STEWART/GETTY IMAGES

BUBBY BRISTER
Seasons with Steelers: 1986-92
Position: quarterback
Height: 6-foot-3
Playing weight: 205 pounds

After the game, Brister met with Cowher and Dan Rooney to discuss his future.

"They came to talk to me right before free agency and said they chose Neil," Brister recalled. "I said if that's the case, I'd like to move on; let me go or try to trade me. They said they would, but they didn't, and this was like February and March and they held me all the way to [June], which I thought was unprofessional. It cost me one of the four starting jobs around the league. I was healthy and had the best four weeks of anybody in the pros. I was healthy and everybody knew it, but they wouldn't let me go."

Instead of working in another team's minicamp, Brister went back home to Louisiana. That's when he met Bonnie.

"That's when I met my wife, so, hey, I'd rather be second team the rest of my career and have a first-string wife and be married and happy and have kids," he said. "Everything happens for a reason. At the time I was bitter, but now I'm happy as I could be."

Brister has been married since 1995. Funny, there was no breaking news bulletin on what had to be the event of the season.

"Everybody I talk to said, 'I can't believe you got married,' and then it was, 'I can't believe you've been married 11 years,' and I say, well, I found the right woman. She's a dark-haired, dark-eyed, beautiful Louisiana girl who loves to cook and is a great mom. She's been singing country and western stuff lately. She's been to Nashville, and I've been supporting her and her career. We're having fun and enjoying—I don't like to say retirement—but being back home and having more time for each other and the kids now that football's over."

The Bristers had a daughter in 1997 and a son in 2001. The daughter's name is Madeline. The son's name is Walter Andrew Brister IV.

"We call him Andrew," Brister said. "No Bubby; no Walter; just Andrew, and he's got a pretty good arm already. I hope he takes after his grandfather. He was also a quarterback and a great baseball player."

Brister, of course, turned down a scholarship offer from Bear Bryant at Alabama to sign with the Detroit Tigers. He played minor-league ball for Jim Leyland before resuming his college football career at Tulane and then Northeast Louisiana.

"My dad was one of best athletes I ever grew up around; even compared with a lot of the kids I played with. He was as good, if not better than any of them. So hopefully Andrew has some of that, and a little bit of me, and hopefully he's a little more calm like his mom."

Brister continues to do public relations work for Ford ("Built Ford tough, just like the Steelers," he pitched with a chuckle) and does hunting and fishing adventure videos for Hunter's Specialties, the top outdoor accessory and game-call company in the world. Brister does a video per month with the company, which has a show on the Outdoor Channel.

"Things are going well with us," Brister said. "My wife has helped me a lot. She went to Philly, New York, Denver, Minnesota, Kansas City, and now we're back home. We were in a lot of different homes in a lot of different years. She was very supportive and helped with the kids when I wasn't there, and now I'm trying to help her some and give her time to do her stuff, and it's working out well."

After the Steelers released Brister in the summer of 1993, he signed with the Philadelphia Eagles as Randall Cunningham's backup. Brister replaced the injured quarterback and in 10 games had his best pro season with an 84.9 passer rating. After two years with the Eagles, Brister spent a season with the New York Jets before moving on to a three-year stint with the Denver Broncos.

Brister won two Super Bowl rings as John Elway's backup. In 1998, Brister replaced the injured Elway and won all four of his starts during the second Super Bowl run. Brister played the next season with Kansas City before retiring after 14 NFL seasons.

His time in Denver was one highlight, but his game against Denver, in 1989, capped his finest series of moments with the Steelers. Off an upset of the Oilers in the wild-card round, the Steelers—behind breakout performances by Brister and Merril Hoge—led the heavily favored Broncos until Melvin Bratton's touchdown put the home team up by a point with 2:24 left.

The Steelers had time for a game-winning drive, but fumbled the ball away when Chuck Lanza's low shotgun snap hit Brister in the shin. Lanza had replaced Dermontti Dawson, who left the game moments earlier with what Brister called "altitude sickness."

"We probably should've taken a timeout," Brister said. "Playing in Denver after that I've seen a number of teams do stuff like that at the end of games because it's so loud and the fans there are so crazy and into the game. You can't hear. That's their homefield advantage, and it's for real."

Brister was happy to win two rings in Denver, but he seems more pleased to have developed a friendship with Elway.

"Rooming with John Elway was unbelievable," he said. "The stuff I learned from him—why he and guys like Michael Jordan are the top of the top because of the way they handle themselves on and off the field. Hopefully I can share some of that with my son. You see how professional they are on and off the field. He's pretty incredible."

Does Brister feel he was shortchanged in his career in any way?

"Not really. If I looked through a crystal ball 20 years ago, and could see where my career would lead me, I would take it. I'm happy and healthy. Financially we're stable. The family's healthy. I won a couple Super Bowls and met guys like John Elway. You could look at it and say maybe, but that's being a little selfish. I think everything worked out pretty well."

CHAPTER 27

Rod Woodson

What's funnier than the Cleveland Browns trading up one spot to draft a tight end instead of Ohio star quarterback Ben Roethlisberger? Well, nothing, really. But the Browns came close on draft day 1987 when they traded up to the fifth spot to select Duke linebacker Mike Junkin. It allowed Rod Woodson to slip to No. 10, where the Pittsburgh Steelers scooped him up in an instant.

"I'm in love with him," Chuck Noll in a rare moment of exuberance.

Woodson became a starter in 1988, was the NFL's Defensive Player of the Year in 1993, became the only active player named to the NFL's 75-year team in 1994, and in 1995 became the only player to tear an ACL and return to play in the same season. Woodson played only 12 snaps in Super Bowl XXX, although he did return to play in Super Bowls with the Baltimore Ravens and Oakland Raiders.

What happened in between, and how Woodson came to move on to those teams, has become a matter of regret for Steelers chairman Dan Rooney, who admitted the loss of Woodson in free agency in 1997 was a mistake.

"Yeah, he did say that," said Woodson from his office at the NFL Network. "That makes you feel better as person, but you have to make the decision what you think is best for your football team. Tom Donahoe and even Bill Cowher, in a sense, made that decision of what they felt was best for their football team at that time."

Woodson, of course, played in Super Bowl XXX for the Steelers after tearing the ACL in his right knee trying to tackle Barry Sanders in the 1995 opener. In the Super Bowl, Woodson pointed to his knee in exultation after defending a pass. It was a response to Michael Irvin, who'd questioned Woodson's speed the week before the game.

Woodson returned to the Steelers in 1996 but played hurt. He made the Pro Bowl, but, by his own count, was beaten on five deep pass plays, three of

ROD WOODSON
Seasons with Steelers: 1987-96
Position: cornerback
Height: 6 feet
Playing weight: 200 pounds

which went for touchdowns. One of the deep plays was a 53-yard catch by Terry Glenn on the first play of the playoff loss at New England.

Woodson had off-season knee surgery to remove a bone chip and scar tissue, and began hearing whispers around the Steelers' offices. That's when Woodson knew the Steelers didn't think the 32-year-old had much left. Woodson turned down the Steelers' first five-year contract offer that averaged $2 million per year. Their second offer averaged $2.7 million over five years but it was packed with "incentives based on unrealistic team performance," according to Woodson, and the bonus offer had been reduced by $500,000. After Woodson turned down the second offer, the Steelers signed Donnell Woolford, 31, for four years at an average of $1.4 million per year, and then drafted Chad Scott in the first round of the draft.

Woodson held a workout for pro scouts in June. He ran 40s in 4.53 and 4.55 seconds (down from his pre-draft combine range of 4.24 to 4.34) and signed a one-year contract with the San Francisco 49ers for $1.2 million plus incentives that took it up to $2.5 million. He left Pittsburgh as a seven-time Pro Bowler and the franchise record-holder for punt returns, punt-return yardage, kickoff returns, and kickoff-return-yardage. He's still the runaway career leader in all four categories, and his 38 interceptions rank fourth in team history. Woodson was a three-time team MVP and the defensive captain when he left.

"When Franco Harris went to Seattle, that was the most difficult," Rooney told the *New York Times* at the time. "But this thing with Rod is right up there. Right up to now I wanted Rod on our team. You can blame it on the salary cap. You can blame it on anything you want. I really wish he was finishing his career with us for a lot of reasons. It hurts."

Today, Woodson says that rushing his recovery to play in Super Bowl XXX was "not the smartest thing to do, but even in retrospect I thought I was going to spend my whole life in Pittsburgh as a player, so I never knew if we'd make it back to the Super Bowl. I never knew I was going to become a free agent and go to Baltimore and play on one of the best defenses, arguably, in NFL history and would win a Super Bowl. I didn't think that and I didn't think I'd come to the Raiders and go to another Super Bowl. So I never knew I would make it to another one and I needed to try to play in that game. I was probably 45-50 percent healthy at that point.

"In '96 I was still sore, and then my Achilles started acting up a lot, just from compensating for my knee and coming back. My Achilles was really sore in '96, but I had a pretty good year. I made the Pro Bowl, and the next year is the year I went ahead and became a free agent. That was for a lot of different reasons, but at times, when you have a strain on the relationship or a friendship, sometimes the best thing to do is just move on. I think it was the best thing for me to do."

Woodson admitted that, "I didn't play my best football in San Francisco. I was still trying to recover from the knee a little bit, even that second year."

In 1998 he signed with the Ravens, and in 1999 he moved to his preferred position of free safety. In 2000 he was a cog in the Ravens' Super Bowl championship. In 2001 Woodson became embroiled in a feud with Steelers receiver Hines Ward. In the first game that season, Ward flattened Woodson with a blind-side block that bloodied Woodson's nose. Woodson found Ward after the game and said he'd get him back.

Before the second game that season, Hank Poteat, whose sister dated one of the Ravens, told Ward the Ravens had a bounty on him. On the second play of the game, Ward drew a personal-foul penalty from Woodson. Ward was later penalized 15 yards for taunting Woodson, and Ward was fined $10,000 by the league. After the game Woodson told Ward that he wasn't involved in a bounty, but that he "didn't appreciate the way I played the game," Ward said. "He called me a dirty player."

The two players resolved their differences because they had the same agent, Eugene Parker, and because Bill Cowher called Woodson and spoke on behalf of Ward.

"He said I would've loved to have played with a guy like Hines Ward," Woodson said. "Once he said that, I understood where Hines was coming from, that he was a hard-working, blue-collar guy who played hard."

That off-season Ward pulled out of Woodson's dealership while Woodson was pulling in. They chatted amicably at a red light for 30-45 seconds and are now friends.

"DBs just don't like being hit by receivers, and he would really de-cleat guys," Woodson said. "He would hit them as hard as a DB wants to hit a receiver when they catch the ball."

Woodson played seven seasons after the Steelers thought he was washed up. He retired after failing a physical with the Raiders in the summer of 2004. He played 17 seasons in the league and stands third on the NFL's all-time list with 71 interceptions. He set NFL standards with 1,483 interception return yards and 12 interception returns for touchdowns. He also tied an NFL record by recovering three fumbles in a game at Heinz Field in 2002 while playing for the Raiders.

Married with five children ages six to 15, Woodson moved his family from the Pittsburgh area to Northern California to work at the NFL Network. He's another analyst who enjoyed the Steelers' run to the championship in 2005.

"When I was playing I kind of wanted them to do bad," he said. "But once I retired I was a Steeler at heart. I spent 10 years there. I got my start in Pittsburgh, knew almost everyone in the front office, the training room and the workout room, but as we got into it, especially as they started doing better this past year, you were objective. I was objective during the year when they weren't running the ball well and when they were 7-5 and playing pretty poorly. And really, all players, if they played a long time in one city, want that team to have success, but you try to stay objective in all of that. You wish them luck and you wish they can do well, like the Steelers did this past year, but if they play poorly, you have to say they played poorly, and then you try to give the reason why they played poorly. But it was fun. It was good to see the Steelers finally pull it together and have one complete season instead of half of one."

For all of his game-turning plays and eye-popping athletic feats, Woodson made two surprising choices as his most memorable plays with the Steelers.

"Probably my most embarrassing play is when Delton Hall was still there. I got an interception at the goal line and I was running it back. Delton and I ran into each other about 50 or 60 or 70 yards down the field, and we both fell down. I got tapped down by a lineman.

"Probably the most disappointing play in my years playing there was when Tim McKyer got beat on third-and-14 when we were playing the Chargers in the [AFC] championship. We lost and they went to the Super Bowl to play the 49ers. That was the most disappointing play in my 10 years there, because I think we had the best team and should've been in the Super Bowl three years in a row.

"The athletes I played with stand out in my mind. People don't agree with me that we should've won the Super Bowl until I start reading off the list of players who were there.

"I also appreciate the tradition. When I first got there Chuck Noll was the head coach, Mean Joe Greene was the defensive line coach, and Mike Webster, Donnie Shell, and John Stallworth were still there. I saw those guys when I was a kid playing and growing up and watching the Steelers win all those Super Bowls. Then I get to Pittsburgh and they're around, and Mel Blount and Lambert and those guys still came around the locker room. It was a treat to see those guys. Donnie Shell was my roommate my rookie year.

"Having that rich history with Pittsburgh, that stood out a great deal at the beginning of my career, and also having been taught by so many great coaches just in Pittsburgh. Chuck Noll was there, and he won four Super Bowls. Tony Dungy was the defensive coordinator when I was there. Tony leaves and John Fox came in to be the defensive backs coach, and Rod Rust came in to be defensive coordinator. He's a defensive guru. He really taught me a lot, Rod Rust. Tony taught me a lot about playing corner in this league and being positive all the time, but Rod Rust really challenged me as an individual to pick my game up and study film and make the game slow down. It becomes easy watching film and studying throughout the week, so when game day comes you just let your talent take over. They left and Chuck retired, and Bill Cowher came in and brought in Dick LeBeau and Dom Capers.

"I mean, just in Pittsburgh alone I was taught by so many great coaches in my 10 years, just teaching me how to play the game, how to be a good professional on and off the field, in the classroom. A lot of times guys don't get one good coach in the league. It's sad to say that, but I got more than enough during the 10 years I spent in Pittsburgh."

CHAPTER 28

Merril
Hoge

Merril Hoge has come a long way. It's not just his health, which he calls "excellent," but his career as an NFL analyst. He's at the top right now, far, far away from the days in Pittsburgh when he was told to keep his mouth shut until called upon.

"It was a tough situation for everybody," Hoge said of joining the Steelers' broadcasting team in 1995. "Myron had been there for so long, he didn't want anybody else in there."

The Steelers were on their way to the Super Bowl that season, and Hoge had this to say: Bu—, a—, thi—, bu—, uh—.

"I couldn't get a word in edgewise," he said. "Look, I was just trying to learn. I wasn't trying to take anyone's job. Mr. Rooney wanted a player in the booth. It was something the Steelers wanted, but it was not received well by Myron. You had to fight your way in, which was hard."

After the 1995 season, the broadcast general manager sat Hoge down and told him they'd iron the situation out. "He said, 'Bill [Hillgrove] will do play-by-play, Myron [Cope] will do the color, and Merril will speak when spoken to.

"That may sound like a slap in the face, but to me it was heaven," Hoge said. "I finally knew when to talk."

Four games into the 1996 season, Shaun Gayle told ESPN he couldn't work there anymore, so ESPN called Hoge and a star was born. He began as a college football analyst and sideline reporter, but was soon doing what he loves most in broadcasting: breaking down and analyzing game film.

"I'm fortunate that the job is very unique and different from most analysts' jobs," said the former Steelers fullback. "Every Tuesday I have all the tape of the games played Sunday and Monday sent to my home from NFL Films, so I'm able to evaluate the league the way I did as a player. There's just no other way to really evaluate it. There's really not. It's allowed me to call some of the greatest

MERRIL HOGE
Seasons with Steelers: 1987-93
Position: factor back
Height: 6-foot-2
Playing weight: 225 pounds

minds in the world at this level and talk to them about football and expand my knowledge and my learning.

"I tap into those brains and learn, and it's really been an exciting 10 years. As much as I appreciated my nine years in the NFL, it's quadrupled since getting out actually. The fan can get all kinds of highlights; the internet gives you all this access; but they're starving for things that are different and will bring them closer to the game and give them a greater understanding while being entertained. That's why our *Matchup* show has taken off to such a high level."

NFL Matchup is a must-see for the serious football fan, but Hoge, of course, is never too serious. For instance, in 2005 Hoge provoked co-hosts Ron Jaworski and Sal Paolantonio by telling them how and why "his Steelers" would pull off one upset after another on their way to winning the Super Bowl. Hoge had fun, but he doesn't want to be tagged a homer.

"People forget that when the Steelers played Denver in the AFC Championship game with Kordell that I predicted Denver,". he said. "It's difficult for any serious analyst to be negative about the Steelers as an organization. They're respected everywhere at all levels; not just by their former players but front-office people of other teams. I feel I look at them objectively. I showed Troy's play his rookie year and talked about some of their problems. I talked about how they shouldn't be throwing the ball so much a few years ago, so I've been as fair with them as any team.

"I know that when I say something good about them it's magnified, but I don't just say they're going to win; I say how they're going to win. Like with the Colts in the playoffs. I was the only one [at ESPN] who predicted they were going to win, and I said how they'd win. After that Monday night game, I knew the Colts wouldn't change. They don't change. But the Steelers had a different game plan, both offensively and defensively. They made adjustments. I just saw too many things in that game that the Steelers were not going to do again. Even though the score didn't indicate it, they whipped the Colts."

For Hoge, the 2005 season went better for him than for his old team, and that's saying something. For one, his recovery from non-Hodgkins lymphoma continued for a third year. He was diagnosed on Valentine's Day 2003 at stage two of the cancer of the immune system. Stages three and four are considered deadly, so Hoge underwent six rounds of chemotherapy and then antibody therapy.

"They usually make you go five years before they consider you cured, but I told them I could've helped them make that prediction a long time ago," he said. "As soon as I got done with my chemotherapy, I knew where I was going. But I've got a couple more follow-ups for a couple more years, and I'll be cured."

What was his reaction the day of the diagnosis?

"I was devastated beyond description," he said. "But through all of that initial darkness, there was a spark inside me, although very little, that I just refused to let this take me. Faith is powerful. The will of a person is powerful. And those two things were at the forefront. As I got information and realized what kind of battle was ahead of me, and learned the treatment was going to be brutal, I ended up having two battles: You battle cancer and the treatment. It's kind of a double whammy, but with the mindset similar to the one I used when I wanted to play in the NFL or when I had to transition to my life's work—as Chuck would say—with ESPN, I had to make my decision. I had to find a way to do it, find a way to get it done, and in that process you find it through faith, will, through other people and through goals. One thing I can tell you is the key ingredient: Every day you must wake up and have that mind-set to attack. Once that becomes habitual, every day becomes routine.

"It was a long six months, but I'm grateful to say physically I was able to persevere through the whole thing. I trained through the whole time. I did my normal routine through the whole thing. Really, the only thing that happened to me was I lost my hair, and that came back. Three years later I use it a lot to keep things in perspective, or to help make certain decisions where you can get caught up in life and lose priorities. When something's critical and you have to make a decision, I reflect back on those emotions going through chemotherapy and wondering if I was going to live to see tomorrow. That helps put things in perspective. So I'm grateful for the challenge. It's not something I want to do again, but it's been invaluable in helping me live life and enjoy life."

So 2005 brought another healthy year for Hoge. He also told the hows and whys of the Steelers' run to the championship. And in a major coup, Hoge crowned Mel Kiper in a draft-day throwdown.

"Mel Kiper and I went at it," Hoge said. "It was probably the greatest draft moment in our draft history. Mel Kiper had Mike Williams as the best athlete on his board, and I'm like, you have no clue. This guy isn't even the best wide receiver, and you have him as your best athlete. If he's No. 1, the kid had better be special, and the kid ain't special. He's not even close to being special. In fact we went at it and he said, 'I'm going to tell you this: Nobody will ever hire you as a scout.' So Mel Kiper, I would like to know, how many people do you think are going to hire you now?"

Hoge believes that his combination of playing in the NFL, his ability (and access) to break down coaching tape, and his interest in college football are helping him become a master of the college draft. Before the 2005 draft, he called Williams and quarterback Aaron Rodgers the most overrated prospects.

Before the 2006 draft, he said the same about quarterbacks Matt Leinart and Vince Young.

"When you make a mistake on any other player, you lose games," Hoge said. "When you make a bad decision on a quarterback, you lose your job. Fans don't realize that. Like in Houston, if I was the owner there, and they drafted Vince Young, I would fire everybody right then and there. I've been doing the draft five years now, and I haven't seen a more dynamic, explosive, special player than Reggie Bush."

Would Hoge want to some day become an NFL personnel man?

"No," he said before laughing. "Matt Millen screwed that up for players like me of ever doing that."

Hoge thinks highly of Kevin Colbert, the Steelers' top personnel man.

"He's made excellent picks, and he's been patient," Hoge said. "They could've panicked on Troy Polamalu. To see where Troy Polamalu is today from where he was his first year is amazing. He's the first player I ever saw on tape, his rookie year, to literally stand there when the ball got snapped because he didn't know what was going on.

"Kevin is a great evaluator, and he's patient. He trusts his eyes; he trusts the people around him; he trusts the tape. If you listen to fans, you'd make mistake after mistake, but if you've done your job, and you know what you're doing, you've earned the right to trust."

As a player, Hoge caught 50 passes in 1988, 49 in 1991 and rushed for 772 yards in 1990. In the 1989 playoffs, he had back-to-back 100-yard rushing games in an upset win at Houston and a near-upset at Denver, in which he compiled 180 yards rushing and receiving. Hoge left the Steelers as a free agent in 1994 and retired after one season with the Chicago Bears.

"A couple highlights that stand out," he said, "were meeting Walter Payton; stepping in the huddle and looking at Mike Webster and John Stallworth; being taught by one of the great coaches of our time, of any time, Chuck Noll; and seeing the growth of another Hall of Famer, Bill Cowher, seeing him in his infancy.

"If I think of games, we had a playoff run there that was truly special. At Houston I scored to put it in overtime and then had a run to put us in field goal range to win it. The Denver game sticks in most people's mind, because everything was so magnified at that point, and it was so close the whole game. It seemed like every play I was able to make was critical. But they came back, and it was one of those games you hate to lose, but when you look back on it, I'd rather have lost and been part of it than not to have been part of it at all."

CHAPTER 29

Dermontti Dawson

Bill Parcells subscribes to the "Planet Theory" that tells NFL personnel men there are only so many big men on the planet who can move well enough to play pro football, and you must draft as many of them as possible.

Parcells had many successes, but Eric Moore was not one of them. That's whom Parcells drafted in 1987 instead of Dermontti Dawson.

"When Ron Erhardt came over from the Giants to become our offensive coordinator," Dawson recalled, "he said to me, 'Daws, we liked you. We were going to take you in the first round, but Bill got cold feet and went with Eric Moore. We should've taken you.'"

The Giants also had a chance to draft Dawson in the second round, but instead took Jumbo Elliott.

Yep. Planet Theory.

"Although I was small," sad Dawson, who came into the league 6-foot-2, 272, "I was strong and fast, which makes up for size. Plus, you can't determine a man's heart. And I took pride in not getting beat. That was my worst fear."

Dermontti Dawson, future Hall of Fame center, was strong, fast, had a big heart, plenty of pride, and was driven by a fear of failure. It's still driving him, still pushing him to succeed at a Hall of Fame level. Dawson struck it rich working in commercial development for the Bellerive Development Company in his hometown of Lexington, Kentucky. He's also started a minority development company.

In the spring of 2006, Dawson and Bellerive were in the middle of another score. They were opening a 92-acre shopping center and 1,100 acres of residential development in Nicholasville, Kentucky.

"I've been blessed," Dawson said. "I've been working with my neighbor, Jim Hughes, who owns Bellerive. When I was playing football I was investing in commercial real estate with his company. He told me to start out small and get

DERMONTTI DAWSON
Seasons with Steelers: 1988-2000
Position: center
Height: 6-foot-2
Playing weight: 288 pounds

a feel for it to see if I liked it. The first thing I did was put a small amount of money in a limited partnership, where you get a guaranteed 10 percent return on your money. But after I started getting those returns back, those disbursements, that became pretty nice. I never thought you could make so much money being in commercial development. Sometimes you make as much as playing football. It's amazing. It's truly amazing, and I have truly been blessed."

Dawson shares the knowledge, and therefore the wealth. He came back to Pittsburgh a few years ago and gave a presentation on some of his projects. Mark Bruener, John Fiala, and Roger Duffy invested and are happier men today because of it.

"I always encourage guys in the league to put their money away, put it in a big institution and put yourself on a budget," Dawson said. "I've been out of the league five years, and I'm making almost the same salary I made in football. It's great to be able to do that and not touch the money that you've worked hard for. Everybody calls on you, wants you to do this, do that, invest in different projects, but unless you know what you're doing and have some general knowledge, and educate yourself, you can lose your money easily."

Dawson has first-hand knowledge of it. He had to sue to recover almost $400,000 that his first agent had swindled.

Dawson invested in the laundromat business during his playing days. He owned three, but sold them early in the spring of 2006.

"That's one less headache I have to deal with," said a man for whom a headache would seem impossible.

Dawson was always cordial during his days with the Steelers. And why not? He stepped in for Mike Webster in 1989 and started 171 consecutive games. He blossomed in the offense Ron Erhardt brought with him in 1992. Erhardt asked Dawson to pull quite a bit, and it was a perfect fit. Dawson made the Pro Bowl every year from 1992 to 1998 and some came to consider him the game's greatest center because of that speed, strength, heart, pride, and fear of failure.

His former offensive line coach, Kent Stephenson, calls Dawson the best center to ever play the game. Chuck Noll, who raved to reporters about one other camp rookie, Jack Lambert, also lavished praise on the rookie Dawson. "I've never seen anyone quite like him, really," Noll said in August of 1988.

Defensive line coach John Mitchell liked to warn rookies about Dawson the week before the vets showed up for training camp. Mitchell would stop a one-on-one drill and say, "Son, if you can't move your hands any faster than that, Dermontti Dawson will put you up against that snow fence when he gets here."

Dawson was a track and field star in high school and almost didn't play football. Bryan Station High won the Kentucky state track and field championship every year during Dawson's time there. He was the undefeated state shot and discus champ in his junior and senior years, and college recruiters told him he could add the javelin and perhaps throw in the Olympics.

University of Kentucky coach Jerry Claiborne spotted Dawson at the state meet his sophomore season. Claiborne called Bryan Station coach Steve Parker and asked why Dawson wasn't on the list of prospects Parker had sent him.

"So my junior year Coach Parker walked up to me in the hallway and said, 'Where've you been all my life?'" Dawson said. "I was the same height I am now and I weighed about 220. I was skinny, but I could run. So he introduced himself, and then had two of my track buddies—Mark Logan and Cornell Burbage—talk to me about playing football. So, we all played, we all got scholarships to UK, and we all played in the NFL.

"I had all these scholarships for track and field, and I'd love to have gone to the Olympics, but you don't make any money in the Olympics from track and field. So I had a scholarship to play football, and I had no intention of playing pro football. I went to UK and they redshirted me my freshman year, and I didn't start at right guard until my junior season."

Dawson played a little center as a sophomore but didn't play the position again until the Senior Bowl. The Steelers liked his versatility, not to mention the 4.8 40 he ran at the combine (Dawson said he was timed earlier at 4.6), and drafted him in the second round in 1988. They drafted Notre Dame center Chuck Lanza in the third round, and the two squared off to fight for Webster's job in 1989. Dawson, of course, won the competition.

"I learned a lot from Mike," Dawson said. "Mike would be in the weight room early in the morning. And even though he'd been in the league 15 years, he wrote everything down just to reinforce and make sure he knew the game plan, what everybody did and what their blocking assignments were. I tried to emulate that. And also, Mike, as soon as he got out of that huddle, he was sprinting up to that line, because you're the leader and it starts with you. I tried to emulate that as well.

"That was my thing: I took pride in making sure I knew what I had to do and what everybody else had to do. You take pride in that. Making no mental errors is something we have control of, and I did not like to make mental errors because coaches don't like that. It shows a lack of concentration."

Dawson's pro highlights range from his first start, when he injured his knee with two minutes left in the fourth game of the 1988 season, to Super Bowl XXX.

"The highlight of my Super Bowl was snapping the ball over Neil O'Donnell's head," he said with a laugh. "I will always be known for that. We all have something, and in the biggest game of the season I snapped the ball over Neil's head.

"It was funny, because you're so engulfed and so tuned in as the center. I had to make the calls, and I'm looking around, talking to guys. I thought Neil was underneath, but I didn't feel his hands, and it was just one of those things, it didn't register, and I snapped it hard and it went over his head. Luckily he recovered it, and we only lost a few yards. They didn't get the ball, thank goodness, and that's the only thing good about it."

Dawson played at a Pro Bowl level until 1999, when he tore a hamstring in the seventh game. He returned in 2000, but because of the hamstring, couldn't get past the ninth game. He retired after the 2000 season.

Dawson and his wife, Regina, are raising their children back home in Lexington, where they have a large extended family. Dermontti calls his daughter Briana "Miss Baseball." She's also in the band. Brandon is playing football and running track. Dermontti is an assistant track coach at Brandon's school.

"He just stated playing football, so it's a learning process for him," Dawson said. "I told him it's going to get easier as you learn your techniques, how to stay low, how to use your hands. He's 5-11, 260 pounds and he's playing defensive tackle, and he's strong. Me being an offensive lineman, I know what defensive linemen do and what's successful and how you can get beat. So I just tell him if you stay high you're going to have a double-team every once in a while. You've got to get low and hunker down."

After all, he wouldn't want to end up over there on the snow fence.

CHAPTER 30

Carnell Lake

It took Donnie Shell four years to make the transition from college linebacker to starting strong safety with the Steelers. Troy Polamalu needed a year on the bench to learn the position, and he was a strong safety in college.

It makes what Carnell Lake did as a rookie in 1989 all the more impressive. Lake made the transition from college linebacker to starting strong safety in one off-season and was the opening-day starter his rookie season with the Steelers.

Lake actually made his first start at strong safety in the 1989 Senior Bowl, and he played well enough to interest the Steelers. But ...

"That projection's not easy to make," personnel director Dick Haley warned, "and it doesn't work very often."

Lake was an outstanding college linebacker. He led the Pac-10 in sacks as a junior, covered tight ends as a senior, benched 330 pounds, and ran a 4.42 40 at the combine, yet at 208 pounds he was too light for the position. Where could he play? His coaches at UCLA promoted him as a running back, but the Steelers drafted Lake with the sixth pick of the second round, 34th overall, to play safety. And Lake was surprised because his favorite childhood team had shown little interest up until then.

"Dick Haley came by UCLA and talked to me maybe two or three minutes," Lake recalled from his home in Jacksonville, Florida. "He just talked to me real briefly, didn't work me out or anything. I had a nice conversation. He just said, 'Hey, it was nice to meet you,' and I didn't hear anything back till draft day."

Did Lake say anything to Haley?

"I mentioned that I had met Mean Joe Greene early on in my childhood because of my godfather, Roy Jefferson," Lake said.

CARNELL LAKE
Seasons with Steelers: 1989-98
Position: strong safety
Height: 6-foot-1
Playing weight: 210 pounds

Hmmm. Perhaps the Steelers had to think long and hard about drafting Lake because Jefferson wasn't a friend of the Steelers, or Noll in particular. He had traded Jefferson away in 1970. Jefferson wasn't exactly friendly toward of the Steelers, either.

"I was a Steeler fan as a child, but I couldn't tell Roy that," Lake said. "We were Redskins fans because of Roy, but in the '70s it was pretty hard not to be a Steeler fan."

Lake's father, Eugene, grew up in Midland, Pennsylvania, and had three brothers and two sisters in the area. Carnell's Uncle Brent played with Simmie Hill and Norm Van Lier on Midland's undefeated 1965 state championship basketball team. Carnell's dad played basketball and football at Midland and went to the University of Utah to play football. That's where he met Jefferson and the two became best friends and took turns babysitting each other's kids. Jefferson nicknamed Carnell "Screaming Sam," because the infant cried every time his parents dropped him off.

After Jefferson went off to the NFL, Eugene Lake moved back to Midland. His wife and two boys went to Los Angeles, where Carnell became a star running back at Culver City High. He went to UCLA as an outside linebacker and was a three-year starter, but Lake was smart enough to realize he'd have to play safety at the next level, so he took lessons from teammate Darryl Henley, a cornerback who showed Lake enough technique "that I could fake my way through workouts until I could get a grasp," Lake said. "And that's what I did."

When Lake reported to St. Vincent College, he "watched Rod Woodson like a hawk," Lake said. "I just sat there and watched everything I could and picked it up like a sponge. And it was good enough to earn me a starting spot my first year."

At the urging of defensive coordinator Rod Rust, Noll cut incumbent strong safety Cornell Gowdy, and Lake had the job. He started in the 51-0 opening-day loss to the Browns and didn't get burned.

"Well, I did get burned. Thanks for not seeing it," Lake said 17 years later. "But in a 51-0 game, even if I did have a bad game, everybody else was having a bad game, too. The fact is I had a great game. They had me covering [Eric] Metcalf a lot, and he was quick as a cat. Not many people could cover him, but I covered him and put some good hits on him. He didn't score a touchdown on me, and I made some tackles in the backfield and I walked away from the game saying I could do this."

Lake learned a lesson in play-action quarterbacking from Boomer Esiason the following week, but his job was secure and he made strides. In a 17-7 win over the Browns, Lake made a spectacular interception, recovered a fumble, defensed two other passes, made five tackles and was the AFC Defensive Player of the Week. By the time Lake played the Kansas City game in the eighth week, Chiefs defensive coordinator Tony Dungy was a fan.

"I really liked Carnell coming out," Dungy told reporter Rick Gosselin at the time. "I saw a lot of Lester Hayes in him. Lester was the same type of guy in college—an outside, walkaway linebacker at Texas A&M. Both Lester and Carnell had great athletic ability and toughness. I thought Carnell would end up at corner, but he's playing really well for them at strong safety."

Smart man, that Tony Dungy, because Lake eventually made the move to cornerback, and it saved the Steelers' Super Bowl season.

Coming off his first Pro Bowl appearance, Lake became the Steelers' emergency left cornerback after the team fell to 3-4 in 1995. Woodson had been injured and opposing quarterbacks could not avoid replacement Alvoid Mays, so Bill Cowher called Lake into his office to discuss a move to cornerback.

"He approached it in a way that I felt like it was my decision, like if I'd said no it would've been OK," Lake said. "But being in the AFC Championship game the year before, I just felt this was something I needed to do to try to get our team in the Super Bowl, and it worked."

After Lake moved to cornerback, the Steelers won their next eight games to clinch the division title. Lake's worst game in the stretch was the 49-31 win over the Bengals, who took a 31-13 lead, mostly at Lake's expense.

"Cowher called me over and told me cornerbacks have to have short memories," Lake said. "That little off-the-cuff remark really stuck with me."

In the playoffs, Buffalo receiver Andre Reed boasted before the game that the Bills would pick on Lake, but Lake intercepted a pass and recovered a fumble in the Steelers' 40-21 win.

Lake played in the Super Bowl and then the Pro Bowl. He made the Pro Bowl again following the 1996 season but was needed for more duty at cornerback in 1997. This time he was moved to replace ineffective rookie Chad Scott. Lake remained at cornerback throughout the 1998 season, when he played on an injured left foot. It was his last season with the Steelers.

"I thought my play was better than it had ever been," he said. "The only problem was I got injured in '98, and that was the year I really felt my cornerback skills were at the top of my game. We didn't have anybody else, and I just wanted to see if I could play through it. I should've stopped to take one or two weeks off, recovered, and come back. Playing injured, you have to do that, but playing hurt is not recommended, and that's the only regret I have because it lingered on even when I went to Jacksonville."

Lake signed with the Jacksonville Jaguars on the first day of the 1999 free-agency period. Tom Coughlin cited his new safety's big play in a 1996 game, in which Lake sacked quarterback Mark Brunell, forced a fumble, recovered the fumble, and returned it 90 yards for a game-clinching touchdown. It was the kind of play Steelers fans had come to expect from Lake, and so had Coughlin. But Lake's foot still bothered him in 1999, and after the season he underwent three separate surgeries. He sat out the 2000 season and came back in 2001 as a nickel back with the Baltimore Ravens. Lake's final game was a playoff game at Heinz Field. He said he received a friendly welcome from fans during pregame warmups.

"I had made a connection with the community," he said. "I was honestly there to try to make a difference in the off-season as well as on the football field. I put my heart and soul into it. I lived there year around and I had relatives there, so it was home to me for a number of years. I just fed off the community because they were cheering for me and they always were warm and welcoming to me. That's what I remember about Pittsburgh."

Lake remains married to Monica, his college sweetheart. They're raising three children, ages five to 10, in Jacksonville. Lake's foot is fine, and he only works on one business project per year.

"The Jacksonville weather is what got me," he said. "Florida's a great place if you're like me and like to be outdoors with your family. I spend a lot of time golfing. I had a good experience with the Jaguars, but the majority of my playing career was with the Steelers and I will always consider myself a Steeler."

Polamalu, the Steelers' current strong safety, is being called one of the more unique players in team history. But how should his predecessor—who made a successful transition from linebacker to cornerback—be remembered?

When Lake left the Steelers, he was second among active team players in both sacks and interceptions, and he credits his position coach and defensive coordinator, who were one and the same.

"Dick LeBeau should be in the Hall of Fame," Lake said. "If they gave assistant coaches a place in the Hall of Fame, he deserves my vote. For somebody who could've been just average or could've been just OK, he made me better. And I think if you ask safeties like Troy, I think he would tell you the same thing."

CHAPTER 31

Jerry
Olsavsky

If Jerry Olsavsky didn't give his heart and soul to the Pittsburgh Steelers, he at least gave his left knee, the one that was blown up one Sunday in Cleveland. But Olsavsky may have given them something else. He may have given them Willie Parker.

Dan Rooney Jr. scouted and signed Parker, but Olsavsky was the assistant strength coach at North Carolina, and Parker was a most serious strength student.

"Willie Parker was a little disenchanted because he knew he could play," said Olsavsky, who reminded Parker that he belonged and to keep working.

"It's difficult sometimes in college to tell a guy to keep plugging away, keep doing what the coach says, and that if you're good enough somebody will find out," Olsavsky said. "I'm so glad the Steelers found out."

Olsavsky, of course, is a Man of Steel through and through. He was born in Youngstown, Ohio, became one of the great tacklers in Pitt history, and gave his heart and soul to the Steelers. He came back from a hit that tore three knee ligaments during the 1993 game in Cleveland to become the team's starting inside linebacker in 1995. He's the classic story of the too-small, too-slow kid who made good because of a big heart. If the Steelers were to ever come up with a Comeback Player of the Year award, it ought to be called the Olsavsky Courage Award or the Jerry O Don't Quit Trophy. But …

"I would call and say no," Olsavsky said. "I don't want that to happen. To me, that was just something I do. If I didn't have Jim Bradley and Chris Harner operate on my knee, and if I didn't have Rick Burkholder and John Norwig help me rehab my knee, and if I didn't have friends support me, and my family. … It's not about me. If I didn't have Tom Donahoe, Bill Cowher, Mr. Rooney re-sign a guy who hadn't played in 400 days. … I used the body that they fixed up.

I just did what everyone told me to do. I benefited more by coming back than they did by bringing me back. It's the best thing that ever happened."

Olsavsky uses the lessons he learned in coaching today. He's back in his hometown working with linebackers and the kickoff team at Youngstown State, one of the top Division 1-AA programs in the country. He and his wife, Rayme, are raising four-year-old Joseph and three-year-old Emma with another on the way. Asking whether he'd some day like to coach with the Steelers isn't necessary.

"People ask me about playing in the NFL, the players, they say how do you do it?" Olsavsky said. "The first thing you have to do is you have to be the best college player you can be. Once you do that, then you can move on. It's the same thing in coaching. I have to be the best 1-AA linebacker coach I can be, and then maybe I can move up.

"It just seems like I've been very lucky my whole life to be in the right place at the right time with the right people. I just trust that."

At a meeting in the spring, Olsavsky told his linebackers they were all better athletes than he was. Olsavsky played college football at 203 pounds as a freshman and 214 pounds as a senior, but in 1988 he became the first Pitt player in 12 years to make 100 tackles in three consecutive seasons. And Pitt was at an elite level from 1976 until Olsavsky arrived.

"I was blessed with a nose for the ball," he said. "I know where the ball is, and I want to get there as bad as anyone ever was taught. That's what helped me."

The Steelers drafted Olsavsky in the 10th round in 1989, and very early Chuck Noll was telling friends that Olsavsky was "special." When Hardy Nickerson broke his ankle in the middle of the season, Olsavsky stepped in, and in his first game stopped 260-pound Christian Okoye, the "Nigerian Nightmare," at the goal line to preserve a six-point win. Olsavsky went on to make 41 tackles in eight games and was voted to several All-Rookie teams.

He was pretty special.

"I've heard that," Olsavsky said of Noll's comment. "I think that's really a term people use when you can't explain instincts or how a guy can make a play. Other people have said that. Joe Moore said that when I was a freshman, that I could make plays. Sometimes that gets lost with younger kids today. They try to make plays. I never tried to make plays, I just made them. I have to credit my coaches when I was young for instilling in me that, hey, you have to get to the football and do everything."

Olsavsky said his coaches at Chaney High—Ed Matey and Ron Berdis—were "incredible." Matey told a Pitt recruiter, in town to see a player from rival Cardinal Mooney, about Olsavsky. The recruiter passed the word along to Pitt Coach Foge Fazio, and said Olsavsky would make every play.

DOUG PENSINGER/GETTY IMAGES

JERRY OLSAVSKY
Seasons with Steelers: 1989-97
Position: inside linebacker
Height: 6-foot-1
Playing weight: 221 pounds

"Take the kid or you're crazy," Matey told Fazio, who took him. Three hundred and sixty tackles later, Olsavsky was with the Steelers.

He got off to a slow start at his first pro training camp. On one particular trap play, Olsavsky was blindsided by Craig Wolfley.

"Flat as a pancake," Olsavsky said. "Then, as we were jogging over to do a pass drill on another field, Chuck jogged by me and he said, 'Hey, that two-trap's a pretty good play.'"

Olsavsky wanted to spit, but he credits Noll with sparking him, and Olsavsky finished the preseason as the Steelers' leader in tackles. He went on to play a key role in the team's torrid finish in 1989. He even blocked a punt in the upset playoff win at Houston.

Olsavsky eventually became a full-time starter in 1993 but suffered an ugly injury—later termed a dislocated knee—while tackling Tommy Vardell at Cleveland in the eighth game of the season.

"With a dislocation," Dr. Jim Bradley told the *Post-Gazette*, "you can lose your leg. It's bad enough sometimes you have to amputate."

The first thing Bradley noticed when he ran onto the field was that the players couldn't look at the fallen linebacker.

"It wasn't pretty," said Levon Kirkland.

"It looked like his knee was sticking straight out," said Darren Perry.

"I'm surprised he wasn't crying," said Donald Evans. "He must be a tough individual."

The tough part came in rehabilitation, and Olsavsky was up for a challenge. "Some people you have to chase to get into rehab," said assistant trainer Rick Burkholder. "Jerry, I had to chase him out."

"If you looked at my career up to '93," Olsavsky said, "you might say, wow, you're tough and you beat the odds. To me, I was just playing football. I wasn't doing anything special. Before I got hurt, everyone said I was such a hard worker, but I wasn't working hard. I was doing what I loved. After I got hurt, then I found out what hard work was about.

"Hey, if I didn't get hurt, I wouldn't be able to put cribs together and stay up all night with babies crying and do things that are really tough. I wouldn't be able to do that. That's hard. But that's what getting hurt taught me: Hey, you've got a lot of ability, now you've got to work.

"Your potential for success is only limited by what you think you can do. If you work at things, you're going to succeed. That's what being hurt taught me. That's why I'm so grateful."

Two tendons from a cadaver replaced two of Olsavsky's ligaments, and after a grueling rehab Olsavsky returned 13 months later. The Steelers gave him a new contract, thick with incentives, and in the first game he made a special-teams tackle. He returned to the sideline and was mobbed by teammates. Tears ran down Burkholder's cheek.

Olsavsky was a reserve behind new starter Chad Brown in 1994, but replaced the injured Brown throughout most of the 1995 season. Olsavsky started the final four games, intercepted a pass in the playoffs and rotated with Brown in the Super Bowl.

In 1996, Olsavsky became the first Steeler to have his salary restructured downward to help the team comply with the salary cap, and he also had his best pro season. Brown moved outside to replace an injured Greg Lloyd, and Olsavsky started 13 games and made a career-high 63 tackles. But in 1997 he lost his job to Earl Holmes, and then Olsavsky exercised an option in his contract to be released after the season. The Steelers tried to talk him into staying, but Olsavsky wanted to start and signed with the Baltimore Ravens for one last season.

"When I look back on things," he said. "I should've made a concerted effort to gain 15 pounds, and then I could've played at 235, and then I would've been more durable and not been hurt as much. Really, I think I could've made a better impact, but when you're young you know you can play, and you fight to stay on the team and that's what happens."

In 2002, Olsavsky assisted the Steelers' coaching staff at training camp. He went to North Carolina as the assistant strength coach and moved on to Youngstown State in 2003.

Olsavsky's best pro memories are of the 1995 and 1996 seasons.

"We were a team and we were tight," he said. "But this last Steeler team was better than the teams I played on because they were so together and they played together and were unselfish and that's who wins the Super Bowl, the most unselfish team. They won it because they were all unselfish, even Jerome. Jerome wanted to get there worse than anyone and have a big day, but who had the big day running the ball? Willie Parker. That's selfless, and to me that's why they won. Joey Porter wanted to do everything. Troy, Ben, they all wanted to do everything, but they sacrificed for the team. You know the defense wanted to win for LeBeau, the team wanted to win for Jerome, the offense wanted to win for Jerome, they all wanted to win for Cowher, he wanted them to win, they all wanted to win for Mr. Rooney.

"No one wanted to win it for themselves. That, to me, is the lesson of that team. If they can keep that going, they have enough talent, great coaches, great ownership, that they can really prove how great the place is."

CHAPTER 32

Levon Kirkland

The 275-pound linebacker left the St. Vincent College practice field to speak to a reporter standing in the end zone. The reporter grew concerned when the approaching linebacker did not respond to waves and smiles.

Levon Kirkland didn't appreciate that the reporter had cut the team in the paper before the coaches had. Kirkland did not raise his voice, but delivered his message and left.

"I do remember that," Kirkland said from his office at Clemson University. "Those players were fighting for their lives. When you put things out there, and a guy reads it, he's going to start believing that, and it'll start affecting his performance."

That's Captain Kirk. But there was a day, a day before he had become the Steelers' captain, when Kirkland felt the urge to speak up and did not.

"We had this meeting about a rap video," Kirkland said of the infamous meeting before the 1994 AFC Championship game. "I mean, we were close and we felt good, but honestly we hadn't done anything at that point. I'm in the meeting thinking: This is not good. We were already planning for something that we hadn't done yet."

Eric Green organized the meeting in order to plan a Super Bowl rap video before the Steelers played the AFC Championship game against the San Diego Chargers. The Steelers were favored by 9.5 points but lost, 17-13. Kirkland believes the 1994 team was the Steelers' best of the decade.

"Our defense, instead of two good cornerbacks, we had three because Deon Figures, before he got shot, played very well for us. And our blitzing package was really dominating, killing people. The offense was clicking on all cylinders, and we felt we had a pretty good team and we felt we had a chance to go to the Super Bowl, but man we really motivated San Diego to play to our level and we gave away too many big plays. We kind of had to learn the hard way how to get to

158

LEVON KIRKLAND
Seasons with Steelers: 1992-2000
Position: inside linebacker
Height: 6-foot-1
Playing weight: 275 pounds

the Super Bowl. Every year was like a step to get to the Super Bowl until we
finally got there."

And the meeting?

"Nobody said anything," Kirkland said. "I guess nobody wanted to buck
the system. That was a big-time mistake on my part."

Kirkland led the Steelers with 10 tackles against the Chargers. He had 100
tackles for the second consecutive season after becoming the Steelers' starting
inside buck linebacker in 1993.

David Little had stepped in for Jack Lambert in 1984 and was replaced by
Kirkland in August of 1993. Kirkland was named captain in 1995 and by the
end of the season enjoyed his finest moment: Super Bowl XXX.

"I think that was my breakthrough game," Kirkland said. "That game really
helped my confidence a lot. Before that time I was doing a lot of things
undercover. You didn't hear a lot about me, because we had so many great guys
on defense. We had Rod and Greg and Kevin and Carnell, and I played next to
a guy named Chad, and we had a great defensive line, so really the job I did was
more so the dirty work and there weren't a lot of highlights.

"When you're stuffing running backs, people don't realize how important it
is until you've got a guy who can't stop the run. Sacks and interceptions are good,
but my position really counted on me stopping the run and covering the tight
end down the field. At the time, it wasn't a very exciting thing to do and I wasn't
getting a lot of pub. People who knew the game and studied the game gave me
my props, but I think playing in that Super Bowl, and playing as well as I did, I
think that really helped get the word out, and it really helped my confidence a
whole lot."

In the Super Bowl, the Steelers were outweighed along the defensive front
by an average of 30 pounds per man, but held Emmitt Smith to 49 yards rushing
and the Dallas Cowboys to 56 total yards rushing. Kirkland was the main reason.
He led the Steelers with 10 tackles. He stopped Smith for a loss on third-and-1
that forced the Cowboys to kick a field goal when they were threatening to run
away with the game early. Kirkland also sacked Troy Aikman on a third down in
the second half. A case could be made that Kirkland was the Steelers' best player
that day.

"Emmitt was a measuring stick at the time," Kirkland said. "If you stopped
Emmitt Smith, and stopped his line, you were doing a tremendous thing, and
that's what we did. Honestly, I never told anybody this, but I played that Super
Bowl a hundred times before I actually played the Super Bowl. I played that
game in my mind, as a kid, so much that I wasn't nervous. I remember feeling

very comfortable and focused. I guess it was something that was going to happen. The only thing that didn't happen is that we didn't win the game."

In the 1996 season opener, Greg Lloyd tore the patellar tendon in his left knee. He missed the rest of the season, and Kirkland's responsibilities increased. He remained on the field on passing downs, and that's when the big linebacker showed why he's one of the unique athletes in the history of the game.

Kirkland led the Steelers with 113 tackles and 17 tackles for loss in 1996, and he led Steelers linebackers with four interceptions and eight passes defensed. In a playoff win over the Indianapolis Colts, the big man ran stride for stride with tight end Ken Dilger to intercept a deep pass. Kirkland also covered Marshall Faulk at times. After the season, Kirkland was named to the Pro Bowl, and a star was recognized.

"In a lot of ways I think I kind of redefined the position a little bit, being a big man like I was and doing some of the things I did on the field was kind of unique," he said.

Kirkland made the Pro Bowl again in 1997. Lloyd was injured in the second half of the season at Philadelphia and contracted an infection soon thereafter. Kirkland regained his three-down status and finished the season with a career-high 95 solo tackles. In the 24-21 loss to Denver in the AFC Championship game, Kirkland made 11 tackles with a sack and an interception.

After the season, Kirkland was ranked the world's 10th best football player by Joel Buchsbaum of *Pro Football Weekly*, but the real payoff was a five-year, $25.3-million contract that included $5.5 million in signing bonus. At an average salary of $5 million, Kirkland was the highest-paid player in team history and the highest-paid linebacker in league history.

However, the length of the contract wasn't fulfilled. The Steelers cut Kirkland in the spring of 2001 in order to pay for free-agent pick-up Jeff Hartings and the new Jerome Bettis contract. The Steelers did try to bring Kirkland back at a reduced rate, but he opted to sign instead with the Seattle Seahawks. He played a year with the Seahawks and a year with the Philadelphia Eagles before retiring.

In his last few years with the Steelers, Kirkland struggled to keep his weight down. What had once made him an athletic anomaly began to slow him down. Bill Cowher complained to reporters about Kirkland when he reported to the 1998 minicamp weighing 303 pounds. And on the first day of training camp in 1999, Kirkland joked with reporters that he was "down to 495" pounds. Kirkland played both seasons in the 280-285 range and was voted Steelers MVP both years by his teammates. He lost 15 pounds in 2000 and enjoyed one of his better seasons in spite of a high ankle sprain.

"People thought I'd be a better player if I weighed less," he said. "But the thing was I never missed a game, I was never out, always dependable, always there, a pretty consistent player, a player who made over 100 tackles each year and really most of my career I played only first and second down. If you look at it that way, you could say this guy really did a great deal."

After he retired from the game, Kirkland dabbled in radio before returning to Clemson to complete his studies. He earned a degree in sociology in 2004 and took a job as the school's coordinator of minority recruitment and initiatives early in 2005.

"I get the word out about Clemson University, particularly to minority students," he said. "I do a lot of writing, and I make visits. I'm just kind of a goodwill ambassador here. I relay my experiences at Clemson and also my experiences overall to students and kind of tell them the benefits of being at Clemson."

Clemson and South Carolina were the only schools to offer Kirkland a scholarship out of tiny Lamar (S.C.) High School. Kirkland entered Clemson as a 205-pounder with a goal of adding 15 pounds every year. He set a Clemson freshman record with 5.5 sacks, and as a sophomore won the 1989 Gator Bowl MVP award against Major Harris and West Virginia. Kirkland was a Butkus Award finalist as a junior, and he left Clemson as a 240-pound outside linebacker who often put his hand down to play defensive end.

Scouts weren't sure how he'd project to inside linebacker, and they weren't impressed by his 4.84 40 speed, so he lasted into the second round. The Steelers had their eyes on Penn State linebacker Mark D'Onofrio, but he was drafted 34th by the Green Bay Packers. The Steelers drafted Kirkland with the 38th pick.

The Steelers moved Kirkland inside as a rookie to learn behind Little and Hardy Nickerson. After Kirkland became the starter, he didn't miss a game the next eight years. For his last six years in Pittsburgh, he was Captain Kirk.

"It's kind of funny that people still recognize the name, recognize me," he said. "It's always kind of humbling when somebody asks for my autograph, or tells me they loved the way I played. You know, when I was covering Super Bowls on the radio, ex-players would tell me how much they enjoyed watching me play. You don't really realize the people you touch and that people really loved watching you play. You don't realize it then, but as I look back on it, I realize it was a really great career."

Kirkland didn't work Super Bowl XL. It was a game that matched two of his three former teams—the Steelers and Seahawks—but he stayed home. One fan wore Kirkland's No. 99 jersey, but in Seahawks colors. Being one of the outnumbered Seahawks fans in Detroit, the fan and his jersey stood out as unique—like the player himself.

"I really was happy for the Steelers, especially Coach Cowher," Kirkland said. "He's worked really hard, and I think he's a worthy coach. I know not all people who are worthy of something always get it, but it was nice to see him do it."

Kirkland married Dr. Keisha Tillman in the summer of 2002. The linebacker and the chiropractor have a daughter named Kennedy. She's not playing football—yet. At a pizza place in Kentucky, the two-year-old was bouncing on a trampoline-like apparatus when she suddenly uncoiled to tackle two unsuspecting boys.

"It was a great form tackle," Kirkland said. "She wrapped her hands around them and had her head in place, everything. It was a perfect tackle, and then she did it again. I guess it was her way of saying hello. Kind of like me."

CHAPTER 33

Kevin Greene

The Steelers' long-haired sackmaster of the mid-1990s is selling real estate in Florida.

Does he like it?

"It's OK. It's given me something to do," said Kevin Greene. "I was blessed to play 15 years in the league, and I don't hurt for nothing or want for anything, but I do miss knocking the snot out of Jim Kelly on *Monday Night Football* in Three Rivers Stadium and tearing Thurman Thomas a new one. You know, I miss that. I miss the adrenaline and the passion of football and the fans.

"So do I like real estate? Does that answer your question?"

It's understandable that Greene misses football, because the game consumed him. When he comes back to coach at various training camps around the league, those camps come alive with his passion. It reverberates, echoes, and is the reason coaches bring him in. They want that passion to rub off on their pass rushers, and Greene understands the importance passion plays in the game.

"One of my favorite memories involved the Buffalo Bills rolling into a *Monday Night Football* game at Three Rivers Stadium," said Greene. "We were having a great day, and I could tell by the end of the first quarter they were overwhelmed. The crowd was rocking. The Steeler fans were just cranking out really loud, so Greg [Lloyd] and I just started yelling at Jim Kelly and Thurman Thomas, just yelling: 'Yeah, do you hear that? Hey, we're coming after you! We're gonna get you! Oh, yeah!' Kelly and Thomas were back there and we were yelling and screaming, just intimidating them.

"That, coupled with the crowd, was working on them. I could look in their eyes, in Jim Kelly's eyes, and Thurman Thomas' eyes, and I could just see they were overwhelmed and they were just lost. The way I read their look, they were like 'Oh, God, what are we doing here? These animals are really, really serious.'"

KEVIN GREENE
Seasons with Steelers: 1993-95
Position: outside linebacker
Height: 6-foot-3
Playing weight: 247 pounds

In 1993, the Bills were on their way to their fourth consecutive Super Bowl appearance when they were ambushed in Pittsburgh, 23-0, in a mid-November Monday night game. The same Monday night game was played at the same point of the 1994 season and the Steelers won, 23-10. The torch of AFC supremacy was passed, and the Steelers played in three of the next four AFC Championship games.

"Those Buffalo games were great, because we totally dominated, just stepped on their necks and twisted our cleats," Greene said. "I remember Kelly stopping his cadence just to kind of listen to us a little bit and gather his thoughts about him. We had him rattled, and Greg was ripping him. I was a little more subdued, but when Greg would get in some of those tirades like that with the opposing team it was just great."

Lloyd was the leader of Blitzburgh, but Greene kick-started the era. He came to the team as a free agent in 1993, and his impact was immediate. The Steelers had allowed Jerrol Williams to leave in free agency, so they signed the 31-year-old Greene to a three-year contract for $5.25 million. As a 3-4 outside linebacker with the Los Angeles Rams from 1988 to 1990, Greene had 46 sacks, but the Rams went to a 4-3. Even though Greene had 13 sacks in two seasons as a 4-3 end, the Steelers believed his niche was in the 3-4. They were right.

In the fourth game of the 1993 season, a 45-17 win at Atlanta, Greene and Lloyd combined for 18 tackles, two sacks, two forced fumbles, a fumble recovery, and a batted pass. Greene had the two sacks, which began a personal streak of seven games with a sack. He finished the 1993 season with 12.5 sacks, but 1994 was his best season with the Steelers. On a Monday night game against the Houston Oilers, Greene's wife, Tara, sang the national anthem, and Greene had two sacks and recovered two fumbles in a 30-14 win. He was named AFC Defensive Player of the Week as the team began a run of 10 wins in 11 games.

The last of those wins was a 17-7 victory over the visiting Cleveland Browns that clinched the AFC Central Division championship. Browns owner Art Modell called it "the most boisterous, loudest sporting event I've ever attended." Greene said he'd never seen anything like it, and at the end of the game he jumped into the crowd to celebrate.

"Maybe that was the first crowd jump," he says today.

The Steelers led the NFL with 55 sacks that season as the nickname "Blitzburgh" became part of the NFL lexicon. Lloyd was voted the team's MVP, but told reporters that he had voted for Greene, who led the team with 14 sacks.

The Steelers' run that season was halted in the AFC title game by the San Diego Chargers in one of the gloomiest losses in team history, but Greene said the worst loss occurred the next season when the Steelers reached the Super Bowl and were beaten by the Dallas Cowboys, 27-17.

"That game will haunt me forever," he said. "There are some games you take with you, and I think there's only one game I'll take with me to my grave, and it's that game. There were two reasons. One, we lost. We lost something I had an opportunity to achieve: the ultimate team championship. The second reason, on a lesser note, individually I did not play my best game. I've had an opportunity to play 15 years, and I've had some really cool games, where I'm really standing out and people can't block me and I'm making plays, causing fumbles, recovering fumbles, wreaking havoc. But this game, for unknown reasons, I was just another body in the pile, so to speak. I had two tackles and maybe two, three hits on Aikman. I really hate that of all the games in my career, that that game was an average game for me. I never looked at myself as an average player. I always looked at myself as being a guy who could make plays, a playmaker. So that haunts me."

A win might've clinched Greene a spot in the Hall of Fame, although he should end up there anyway. Greene ranks third on the NFL career sacks list with 160. He led the league in that department twice and is the all-time leader at his position, well ahead of the 3-4 prototype at outside linebacker, Lawrence Taylor, who had 132.5 sacks in his 13-year career.

Greene also ranks third all-time in fumble recoveries and was voted to the All-Decade Team of the 1990s. And even though he was one of the best pass-rushers in NFL history, Greene wasn't a one-dimensional player.

"Kevin Greene is a great player against the run," Dick LeBeau once said. "I think he's one of the best outside linebackers I've ever seen."

So why hasn't Greene received more consideration from Hall of Fame voters?

"I really don't know why," he said. "If the Hall of Fame voters can't just look back on the sheer numbers and production of my career, if they can't look back and say, 'He was productive, one of the most productive linebackers in history.' If they can't do that, then I don't deserve to be in there. I'm holding out hope, but I don't live my life day after day thinking about it."

Greene was named to five Pro Bowls, and two of those Pro Bowls were played during his three seasons with the Steelers.

"It was a magical time," Greene said. "When I look back, the three most magical years of my career were in Pittsburgh."

Greene married Tara in June of 1993, and the couple fit right in with blue-collar Steeler Nation. After games they'd cruise the parking lots in their SUV to chat up postgame revelers. One time, the Greenes brought 100 Big Macs and 100 orders of French fries to fans who'd camped overnight to wait in line for playoff tickets.

"We put down the tailgate and started handing it out," Greene said. "I told them we appreciated them standing out here for tickets to watch us play, and now please share the food; please, don't bogart the food. And you know what? I was passing out Big Macs and people in the front were taking them and passing them back six, seven, eight rows, so nobody in front of me was getting four or five Big Macs and scurrying out. It was amazing. I just met somebody a couple months ago in an airport, and he said he was one of the guys that got a Big Mac and he wanted to thank me. That was so cool. So many years later they remember the Big Macs and the fries."

When Greene's contract expired, Bill Cowher discussed with Greene the possibility of returning as a backup and mentor for young Jason Gildon. Greene, though, had four productive years left, maybe more. He led the Carolina Panthers and the NFL with 14.5 sacks in 1996. In his final season, 1999, he had 12 sacks.

"I was 37 and had 12 sacks. Do you think they figured out how to block me?" Greene asked. "But there was no way I could've found a team able to pay me fair-market value based on productivity. That, I think, is mainly why I retired."

In 2006, the Greenes were raising nine-year-old Gavin and seven-year-old Gabby. Kevin had visited three different camps in 2003, 2004, and 2005 to work with pass rushers. At the Steelers camp, his enthusiasm was obvious, if not contagious, but he said he enjoys his family time too much to pursue a career in coaching. "Maybe later when my kids are older," he said.

Greene enjoyed a brief pro wrestling career that began on an off-day during the week of Super Bowl XXX, but he got out of it because football was his priority.

"It would seem natural for me," he said of pro wrestling, "because I'm a natural nutcake."

Greene was a captain in the Army Reserve, where he was a paratrooper and drove tanks. His father was a colonel in the Vietnam war, and his brother is a Gulf War vet. Greene recently had paratrooper wings tattooed on his left shoulder.

"It's the only tattoo I have, and it kind of shows you how proud I am of my country and the time I spent serving my country," he said.

The pride in his old team swelled when he watched the Steelers win Super Bowl XL. He was happy for his old coaches and happy for the city.

"Part of my heart bleeds black and gold," Greene said. "The memories I have of playing in Three Rivers Stadium, man, and really rolling over people with those great defenses, those are memories that I cherish."

CHAPTER 34

Darren Perry

As a star athlete at Deep Creek High in Chesapeake, Virginia, Darren Perry played football, basketball, and tennis.

So, which word doesn't belong in that sentence?

"I was a pretty good tennis player," Perry said with a proud smile.

The basketball coach told Perry that tennis would improve his hand-eye coordination, so the all-state quarterback took the game up. He's just now finding people to play with him.

"I have four girls," Perry said. "They're big-time tennis players right now. My 13-year-old can beat me. It won't be long for my 10-year-old. I wasn't the best, but for her to beat me at this age says something about her. She might have a chance."

She might have a chance. If Perry sounds like a coach, well, he is. Super Bowl XL ended Perry's third season as an assistant coach with the Steelers. He was the team's free safety from 1992 to 1998 and returned as a coach in 2003. Perry was promoted to secondary coach in 2004, or right about the time the Steelers took off.

"Well, you know it's ultimately all about the players," Perry said with a chuckle.

What's his role?

"As a coach you're dealing with game-planning and really dissecting the opponent in all facets, not just your particular job," he said. "You're trying to look at the big picture. You're trying to get into the opponent's head, but you're also trying to get into your players' heads, in terms of wondering how much can they handle. Will Troy be able to play this defense versus Chad Johnson? Is Ike Taylor our best matchup for Chad Johnson? Are you putting your players in the right position to succeed? That's what coaching's all about."

DARREN PERRY

Seasons with Steelers: 1992-98

Position: free safety

Height: 5-foot-11

Playing weight: 196 pounds

Bill Cowher and Dick LeBeau seek input from their assistant coaches, but sometimes those Tuesday meetings mean little. The game plan is drawn up, and the team devours it, but one series on Sunday can lay the plans to waste. It happened in Indianapolis in the 2005 playoffs.

"We were talking coverage techniques and how we wanted to play a particular route, and we sat there Tuesday and spent hours on how we wanted to play Marvin Harrison," Perry said. "We get in the game and it was, 'Uh, no, let's not do that.'"

On the Colts' first series, Harrison had two steps on linebacker Larry Foote over the middle and was heading up the field but the pass was overthrown. On the next play, Harrison was covered by free safety Chris Hope, who ran into the receiver before batting the pass away. Pass interference was not called, and the Colts punted, but the Steelers didn't like what they were seeing and scrapped their coverage plan.

"It just didn't play out like we envisioned on the board," Perry said. "Our players didn't have a problem adjusting. They were OK with it, and we went on to play one of our best games."

Harrison caught only three passes in the Steelers' 21-18 win. The Steelers were 10-point underdogs, and the upset spurred them to the title.

In the Super Bowl, Perry and the defensive coaches had another problem: Troy Polamalu injured his ankle in practice and wasn't 100 percent. Polamalu had been an important chip for the coaches, and his success was based largely on his speed, but the coaches didn't panic and made the right call: They left Polamalu alone.

"We didn't adjust," Perry said. "He was hurt; or rather he was hurting, if you will. I know he probably wasn't 100 percent, but we didn't change anything to keep him out of certain situations. He just fought through it and did the best he could."

Know when to coach 'em; know when to leave 'em the hell alone.

"These guys are the greatest guys to coach. They really are," Perry said. "All of them—their attitude, the way they approach the game—make my job, the greatest job, so much easier.

"I was a little biased to the group I played with, but I've never been around a group of guys, from top to bottom, that have been as close as our entire roster. I've never seen anything like it. I mean, unbelievable. Unbelievable. I mean, this is the closest group of guys I've ever been involved with as a player and as a coach. It speaks a lot about them."

Perry played with a close group. They called him "Papa Smurf" after his first child, Danielle, was born. Perry stepped into the lineup on opening day as a rookie and didn't come out until the 1997 season, when he missed his only two games in seven seasons with the Steelers.

Perry returned to the lineup and completed the 1998 season, his first and only losing season since joining the Steelers as part of Cowher's first draft class.

The free safety position in Cowher's 3-4 defense is fabled for its complexities. The man at that position must be half Albert Einstein, half Jim Thorpe. That's why the position was a natural fit for Perry, an underdrafted but productive ballhawk out of Penn State.

Of course, this eighth-round draft pick had a wide-open path to the job in 1992. Thomas Everett was holding out, and the Steelers eventually traded him to Dallas for a fifth-round draft pick (Marc Woodard). Everett's replacement, Gary Jones, tore a knee ligament at a training-camp practice, so up stepped Perry. He intercepted Warren Moon in the opener, intercepted Ken O'Brien in the second game and went on to lead the Steelers that season with six interceptions. Perry was the unanimous choice for the Joe Greene Great Performance Award as the team's best rookie.

So much for the vaunted complexities of playing free safety in Cowher's 3-4 fire-zone defense.

"The thing you have to remember about my rookie year," Perry said. "This system was new to everybody, so we were all on equal playing fields. If I didn't know it, chances are no one else knew it either."

After dipping to four interceptions in 1993, Perry found Vinny Testaverde in 1994. Perry intercepted the Browns' quarterback three times in a 17-10 Steelers win at Cleveland. Perry intercepted Testaverde again in the playoffs. Overall, Perry intercepted Testaverde five times with the Steelers as Perry compiled 32 interceptions before he left Pittsburgh following the 1998 season. He's tied with Jack Ham for seventh place on the team's all-time list.

Perry added three interceptions in his final season with the New Orleans Saints, and in 2002 he took up coaching under LeBeau at Cincinnati. Both coaches, of course, won their first championship rings with the Steelers. Obviously, anyone smart enough to play free safety for the Steelers is smart enough to coach it.

"The position's not easy, put it that way," Perry said. "I'm not the smartest guy in the world, but at the same time it takes time. It doesn't happen overnight."

The problem, though, is Perry lost his two-year starter when Chris Hope became a free agent in the spring of 2006.

"We've got a guy that we think can handle it," Perry said. "Ryan Clark's a smart guy, and we feel comfortable with him coming in and being able to keep things going."

"Papa Smurf" and his wife, Errika, and daughters—Danielle, Dominique, Dedriana, and Devan—live in Wexford. The girls play tennis and bug their dad about the games. They're at an age when they're becoming aware of what the team means to the community.

"They're reminded of it when they go to school," Perry said. "Now it's like, 'Dad, who you guys playing this week? Do you think you'll win?' So there are some emotions that come with it. They're starting to understand the losing part of it. It's all a learning experience for them."

Losing wasn't a problem in 2005. What did winning the Super Bowl mean to Perry?

"You've reached the pinnacle," he said. "Everything you do, from training as a player, and as a coach preparing and talking to your guys, drafting, evaluating college guys, all those things that you do, revising the playbook, all the little things you do, it's all geared to winning the championship. So many times you fail, you come up short, and it's like, OK, well, back to the drawing board. Let's keep doing it. Let's keep doing it. So you're chopping wood and chopping wood, and then all of the sudden, boom, you chopped down the tree. And it's like, whoa, we did it. And it was everything they said it was going to be, probably a little more. It was truly an exciting feeling, unbelievable, the sense of accomplishment and the joy you saw not only in the players' faces but your family's and everyone that you've been involved with who are sharing it with you. It's an incredible feeling, the city, the fans, so many outside factors that all have an influence on your perception and how you feel about doing it.

"Everybody now wants to see the ring. You don't mind it because you're the world champs. It's not like high school when you won the district, or you won the state championship, you're the world champs. That in itself says everything."

CHAPTER 35

Ben Roethlisberger

It was back in April of the year of Ben Roethlisberger's discontent when those who supported the Steelers' quarterback and those who opposed him took up their sides and dug in. Troy Polamalu, the conscience of the team, was asked which side he was on.

"Well, I think if Ben has shown anything he's shown he's able to recover whenever he's been faced with adversity," Polamalu said. "I think, regarding this situation that he's going through currently, that'll be the great example.

"Everything's not always peachy, and not everybody has that unblemished image, but I think for him to have that repentance, the way that he's going to have to continue to live his life is going to be the great example – I think a better example than what somebody else could provide."

Polamalu was looking forward to what lies ahead for Roethlisberger. Polamalu knew that everyone would be watching. He knew the 2010 season would be the perfect stage for redemption.

Well, Roethlisberger got his redemption. He got it on the field by taking the Steelers to yet another Super Bowl. He got it from his teammates who rallied around him all season. He got it from the media who voted him the Chief Award for his cooperation. And he got it from his family, when early in Roethlisberger's rehabilitation process his father Ken exclaimed, "I've got my son back."

Ken Roethlisberger was a quarterback himself and was recruited by Georgia Tech to play the position, but instead became a baseball pitcher. He married a girl named Ida and the two moved to Elida, Ohio, where Ida gave birth to Ben.

The couple divorced when Ben was two years old, and Ken remarried. Ben lived with Ken and his stepmom Brenda and saw Ida on weekends. But one weekend Ida didn't make it. She had been killed in a car accident while driving to pick Ben up. He was eight years old at the time.

The Roethlisbergers moved a few miles northeast in Ohio to Findlay when Ben was in the fifth grade. He went out for the midget football team and the coach at the time, Tony Iriti, asked Ben what position he'd like to play.

"He said, 'I'd like to be a running back," recalled Iriti. "So my son Mike was the quarterback and Ben was the running back. We're about three games into the season and of course you've always got to have that trick play, and so I asked Ben if he could throw the ball, and Ben said, 'I think so.' And so I told Mike to pitch it to Ben and for Ben to take about three steps, stop, and throw it back to Mike going down the sideline. And so of course he hits him right in stride going down the sideline. So I said, 'Ben, you are now the quarterback and Mike you are the receiver.'"

And a star was born.

Roethlisberger did have to take a temporary backseat at the position to another coach's son as a junior in high school, but in his senior season Roethlisberger returned to his natural position and led Findlay to its second playoff berth in school history.

Roethlisberger's stint as a high school receiver may not sit well with Findlay historians, but Steelers fans are grateful that the move hid Roethlisberger's talents from the larger schools, and in turn allowed him to fall to pick No. 11 of the first round – past the Kellen Winslow-drafting Cleveland Browns – and into the lap of the Steelers.

"Exactly," said Iriti. "He'd have never played for the Steelers, so it all worked out."

Roethlisberger was a three-sport star at Findlay, and those were the three sports – baseball, basketball, and football – that his father Ken had favored as an athlete. And Ben excelled at every sport due to a wicked competitive streak that is said to have come from his mother Ida.

"I played ping pong against him one time," said hometown friend Tim Tagliapietra. "He had no mercy. One time he played left-handed and he was laughing at me and I was playing my ass off right-handed. Things like that made you realize, hey, maybe this guy's got it.

"He's probably stronger mentally than he is physically, and he's pretty physically gifted."

"I am ultra-competitive," Roethlisberger said during a break from the mob interviews before Super Bowl XLV.

"I'm one of the most competitive people you'll meet. I love to win. I'm not one of those guys who'll let you win because I feel bad for you, or you like my sister. I'm not going to let you win.

"As for whether that's a good thing or bad, I think you've got to find the fine line before you start playing, or before you start doing whatever it is you're going to do, but as a pro athlete people expect you to be competitive."

Roethlisberger, of course, was criticized by some in his hometown during the media frenzy that followed the temporary sexual assault allegation made by a college girl in March of 2010. Investigators couldn't find the slightest trace of DNA, and the girl – videotaped changing her story – dropped the allegation a few days later. But that didn't stop reporters from sorting through Roethlisberger's various stomping grounds – including his hometown – in search of juicy tales. Soon thereafter, Roethlisberger contacted the Steelers and had them change the hometown listed on the roster from Findlay to Cory-Rawson. It appeared that Roethlisberger had a grudge against his hometown. But he says otherwise.

"No, I just wanted to show some love to the elementary school I went to," he explained. "I still have a lot of love and support back home. My church family is still there and I still have a couple friends there. So, no, I don't have any resentment."

Before leaving his hometown for college, Roethlisberger actually hoped to secure a basketball scholarship. ("It's still my love," he said. "I still love basketball.") And when he accepted Miami (Ohio)'s football scholarship, he inquired into the chance he could double as a basketball player.

"Coach [Terry Hoeppner] was like, 'Do you think that's really the smart thing to do? Look at the opportunity you have with football.' So I credit him with keeping me on this path," Roethlisberger said.

That wasn't the only time Roethlisberger mentioned Hoeppner prior to Super Bowl XLV, or any of the three Super Bowls in which Roethlisberger has played. Hoeppner has been a guiding force in Roethlisberger's life. The quarterback went so far as to call his late college coach "a father to me," when Roethlisberger was asked for what Hoeppner would've said about his behavior during the infamous 2010 incident.

"Exactly the same things that my dad did to me and said to me would have been the exact same things that he did. I still talk to Mrs. Hoep and coach's son Drew and the family. It would have been nice to have him here and have another supporter and mentor, but I know he's still looking down and being the best up there."

Even though Roethlisberger started only one year at quarterback in high school, Hoeppner immediately installed him as the starter at Miami and

Roethlisberger set all of the school's passing records before leaving for the NFL following his junior season. In his final season, Roethlisberger led Miami to a No. 10 national ranking and a win in the GMAC Bowl.

The game was watched in Pittsburgh by, among others, Steelers scout Mark Gorscak, who told this reporter – seated next to Gorscak and touting Roethlisberger as the next Jim Kelly – that "he looks more like John Elway to me."

A few months later, in April of 2004, Roethlisberger was in Pittsburgh explaining to reporters that he chose No. 7 because of his affinity for the play of one John Elway as a child.

It took Roethlisberger a little longer to break into the starting lineup in Pittsburgh than it did in college – about a week longer. Starter Tommy Maddox was injured in the Steelers' second game and Roethlisberger stepped in and hasn't stepped out.

Roethlisberger's rookie season was a whirlwind. He smashed the rookie record by winning 13 consecutive games as a starting quarterback. He extended the streak to 14 in the first round of the playoffs, but it came to an end the following week when the New England Patriots – buffed by the illegal videotaping of defensive signals – beat the Steelers in the AFC Championship Game.

That was one of only three playoff losses for Roethlisberger among the 13 he's started through Super Bowl XLV.

While Roethlisberger might not put up the yardage numbers that seem to carry so much weight with NFL public relations, he has the third best all-time post-season winning percentage (10-3/.769) – behind Bart Starr (9-1/.900) and Jim Plunkett (8-2/.800) – of quarterbacks with at least 10 starts.

Prior to the 2011 season, Roethlisberger also held the fourth-best all-time winning percentage (.704) in regular-season games among quarterbacks with at least 90 starts.

In his short time in the league, and through the roughest patch a developing quarterback endures, Roethlisberger has been a winner.

"I know every time we're in the fourth quarter he's not going to quit," said receiver Hines Ward. "We always have a chance to win games. I'll take that over all of them. I wouldn't trade him for any other quarterback out there."

The sentiment has been echoed by Roethlisberger's offensive coordinator since the 2007 season.

"I'm not trading him for anybody in this league," said Bruce Arians.

"And I coached Peyton [Manning]. I love Peyton to death. But in the fourth quarter of a ball game right now in this league, I'm taking Ben to win the ball game."

Over Brady?

"Over all of them," Arians said. "He's done it too many times. You know, that drive he had in Super Bowl XLIII was historic. I was one of the few people who couldn't believe he didn't get the MVP, because the drive that he put together to win that game was an MVP-type drive. Tone [Holmes] made some great plays on that drive, but I think that throw was a little harder than that catch. I'm a little biased, and I was happy for Tone, but that solidified (Ben) to me because that's the biggest stage there is. We get a holding penalty on the first play and he had to go 90, you know. The guy just never loses his cool."

Arians was the Steelers' wide receivers coach when Roethlisberger joined the Steelers in 2004. And Arians viewed him as did most: as a cocky, uncoachable, undisciplined quarterback who'd never learn the NFL disciplines required of a true pocket passer.

Right?

"Oh, no," Arians said. "I just thought 'Wow, what a talent.' I didn't coach him in my room, so it was a different relationship then. I had enough to worry about with my group with Plax [Burress] and Hines and [Antwaan Randle] El, but I saw an ungodly talent who had a great passion for the game.

"When I became coordinator and he became my quarterback, all I asked him was to work as hard as he possibly could because I'm going to give him freedom to run the show and really change what we'd been doing as far has his role, and his role was just play quarterback on the plays called. I wanted him to be able to audible, change plays, have a bigger hand in the game. He helped me re-write the playbook and so that part of it changed and it's just grown from there. I have total, total trust in him."

Roethlisberger can throw from the pocket, but since Marvel Smith, Alan Faneca and Jeff Hartings left the team early in Roethlisberger's career, the quarterback has had to endure several new editions of the Steelers' offensive line.

At the start of the 2010 season, what was thought to be a near-finished product again needed help when right tackle Willie Colon was injured and then left tackle Max Starks got hurt. And then, before the Super Bowl, super rookie center Maurkice Pouncey was injured.

In fact, the only holdover that day from the previous season's starting line, left guard Chris Kemoeatu, was beaten early in the game by journeyman tackle Howard Green – he of two NFL sacks since entering the league more than eight years prior.

Green beat Kemoeatu and crashed into Roethlisberger's right arm as the quarterback was throwing. The ball fluttered into the hands of Packers safety Nick Collins, who returned it 37 yards for a touchdown and a 14-0 Green Bay lead.

Roethlisberger was intercepted again as the Packers pushed their lead to 21-3, but the Steelers scored a pair of touchdowns to cut the deficit to 21-17. However, the Steelers couldn't get over the hump. They started three possessions in the third quarter with a chance to take the lead, but all three drives ended unsuccessfully.

The Packers finally took advantage with a touchdown drive early in the fourth quarter after Rashard Mendenhall had fumbled on a 2nd-and-2 play at the Green Bay 33.

Roethlisberger did complete 7 of 8 passes to drive the Steelers 66 yards for a touchdown, and the 2-point conversion brought them to within 28-25.

Trailing 31-25, Roethlisberger was presented with another chance to duplicate his heroics of Super Bowl XLIII.

Against the Cardinals, Roethlisberger overcame a Kemoeatu holding penalty that backed the Steelers up to their 12-yard line with 2:07 to play before commencing that historic drive. But, against the Packers, lightning didn't strike twice.

Backed up to their 13 with 2:07 to play, the Steelers could manage only one first down before Roethlisberger threw incomplete to Mike Wallace on third and fourth downs to end the game.

"I feel like I let the city of Pittsburgh down, the fans, my coached and my teammates, and it's not a good feeling," a distraught Roethlisberger said after the game.

While he missed a chance for his third Super Bowl ring in his first seven years in the NFL, Roethlisberger was fitted for another ring: a wedding ring. He announced his engagement to Ashley Harlan shortly after the game. And most of those he felt he had let down by losing on the field took solace in reading the next chapter of Roethlisberger's fight for redemption off it.

CHAPTER 36

Hines Ward

As Hines Ward walked slowly and victoriously up the stairway leading to the Steelers' locker room after a December win over the Cincinnati Bengals, his coach, Mike Tomlin, held open the door and called to his star flanker.

"Come on Ol' Yeller," Tomlin said. "I ain't gonna take you out back and shoot you today; maybe tomorrow."

Ward sheepishly flashed his million-dollar smile and slipped in with a pat on the head.

Good boy.

"He likes to mess with me," Ward said later. "But I'm not even the oldest guy on the team."

He was a bit defensive, but he was right. At that point in the 2010 season, Ward, at 34, was the third-oldest Steeler. But he didn't play like it on this day. In the Steelers' 23-7 win over the Cincinnati Bengals, Ward hauled in 8 passes for 115 yards.

Ward didn't play like his age, nor does he dance like his age, as Steelers fans watching top-rated TV dance shows found out during the off-season.

No, it was just another day, another season, another year in the life of Ward, the Steelers' all-time leading receiver.

"It doesn't bug me, it's just perception," Ward said of everyone, even his coach, piling onto the age thing.

"People think that when you get older you start to fall off, which is normally the case. I guess it's something he uses to motivate me, but I have self-motivation already."

Ward had that self-motivation at the ready on the first day of training camp. It was apparent when the simple topic of stadiums was brought up to Ward by reporters. Ward answered that he's "played in every stadium in the league, except the new one in Dallas."

When he smiled, the reporters needed no further explanation because they knew that "the new one in Dallas" is where the next Super Bowl would be played.

It was clear even in late July of 2010 that the Steelers' veteran leader was transfixed on a third Super Bowl appearance in six years.

The next day at St. Vincent College, Ward took the first step in getting the team there. It was to be the first public practice of training camp and quarterback Ben Roethlisberger was to face the fans for the first time since he'd been accused – temporarily – of sexual assault. The media had filed countless stories with numerous examples of Roethlisberger's boorish behavior, so no one was sure how the fans would react that day. But Ward stepped up and helped the teammate with whom he'd shared a hot-and-sometimes-cold relationship throughout the years.

"We're like big brother, little brother," Ward later explained. "Sometimes you get on each other's nerves, but we've never had bad feelings."

This moment was bigger than their relationship. This moment was about the coming together of a team, and Ward seized it.

"All day that was the big thing: How would the crowd respond to Ben on his first day, and he was actually nervous about it," Ward said. "I read some of his quotes. He was sitting on the table waiting to go out, and I said, 'Ben, wait, let me walk out with you. If they boo you, they're going to boo me too and they're going to boo this organization.'

"So we walked out there together. I wasn't trying to do it for media points. For someone who's like a brother of mine, I didn't want him to go through that pain of him thinking we didn't have his back. So I walked out there with him. We didn't hear any boos. The guy made a mistake. We all make mistakes in life. We moved on. Hopefully the fans moved on. I think everybody has.

"Football's an escape, a place where we can go to not think about all the issues that go on off the field, and he's done a great job of doing that and becoming a better teammate, a better person. He's done all that. It's just a great remarkable story to see how we started the year, and here we are with a chance to win a third Super Bowl."

The Steelers didn't win that third Super Bowl, and really no one could blame Ward. In fact, many Steelers fans questioned why Ward was a mere decoy on the final two downs of the 6-point loss after catching 7 passes for 78 yards and a touchdown in the game.

But Ward didn't point fingers nor question the playcalling. For him, it's always been about team. He was that way as a child – one often left to his own devices – of a single, hard-working parent in the south Atlanta suburb of Forest Park, Georgia.

"When we were younger," said childhood friend Corey Allen, "he was the one who picked everyone up and took us to practice. His mom worked hard enough to get him a car, which was always funny to me. She worked two jobs and was never home, but she had enough money to get him a car. So he was one of the first kids in our neighborhood to have a car. But he wouldn't go out and hang out with us. He was taking us to practice. He was making sure we were all where we were supposed to be. He's always been a real good ringleader. He's always been very focused and driven, especially in sports."

Ward was born in Seoul, South Korea, to an African-American father and Asian mother. The family moved to Atlanta when Hines was an infant, but his parents divorced and Hines went first with his father to Monroe, Louisiana, and then back with his mother, Kim Young He, to Forest Park when he was seven.

While his mother worked her multiple jobs until the wee hours of the night, Ward finished school with a perfect attendance record and played every sport he could. He met his close friend – and future college roommate – Allen on a baseball field when they were 12. And Allen thought baseball was Ward's best game at the time.

"He became one of the best center fielders I ever played with," Allen said. "Fast, could cover the field, and he could hit like gangbusters. He had an open stance in front of the box so he was basically facing the pitcher. He hit a lot of home runs, but he had great speed, too. Anytime he got on base, consider him on third."

"I grew up a baseball player," Ward said the week of Super Bowl XLV. "I always played football, but I loved baseball more than I did football. Yet, football was just natural to me. You played pickup football and you learned all your moves. In high school I had a defensive mentality. I was the starting quarterback and the strong safety, rover, linebacker in our group. I was the quarterback and I was laying some devastating blows on tacklers and running backs at the same time. Right then and there I found I loved everything about football. It was fun to me. You get tackled; you get up.

"The biggest challenge when I was a kid was throw-up tackle. I loved that. You'd throw the ball up and get the ball and go against five different guys and try to score. And then when you scored, you felt like you were the king, on top of the world if you can beat five guys to get in the end zone. That's when I really fell in love with football and I never looked back."

He loved it so much, no one could wipe the smile off his face.

"I hated playing against him," said Allen. "One time, as a ninth-grader in JV ball, I told my teammates, 'Look, he played quarterback the year before. They're going to throw the halfback pass.' He was playing tailback in this game. He had probably 150 yards rushing. He was killing us. I was at safety on one side of the field. Fourth quarter, we're up three points, and of course 40 yards in they throw the halfback pass. We all bit on the fake. He's laughing, and you could see him smiling the whole time. That still bothers me to this day, that when you played against him he's laughing the entire time. You can literally hear him laughing and joking. He never liked a mouthpiece so you can always see that Cheshire cat smile, and that just used to irk me whenever I played against him. I hate to see that smile. It's a nasty little smirk."

The smile was there when Ward was drafted to play baseball by the Florida Marlins in 1994, but he instead accepted a scholarship to play football at the University of Georgia. He went with Allen, but he almost left – alone.

Ward went to Georgia as a quarterback, but moved to running back and then wide receiver to help a team that was perilously thin at both positions. In fact, Ward was such a valuable player at each stop on the depth chart that he didn't play a snap in a game against Clemson his sophomore year. So he looked into transferring, and came close.

"Very close. Very close," said Ward. "It was like you're the best player, but you're being unselfish and moving around to all the positions because you're trying to do what's best for the team. But you weren't able to get in games. It was like I'm so valuable being the backup because I was next in line at quarterback, running back and I couldn't go to my natural position of wide receiver because if I took a hit and went down then we don't have any backups. It was a low point in my life. I was almost on my way. My mom, she supported me. We sat down and really talked about it.

"Sometimes change isn't good though. I'm an emotional guy and you really don't want to make a major decision like that based off emotions. I've learned that over the years. You just have to sit back, breathe a little bit, and just wait things out. Everything will play itself out, and it did for me."

There were a few more of those moments in the NFL as well, but Ward managed to use each as motivation.

First of all, he was drafted with the last pick of the third round by the Steelers. Once he got used to that, after he showed as a rookie that he could catch a few passes (15) and blow up opponents on special teams, the Steelers drafted another receiver, Troy Edwards, in the first round. And after Ward broke out with 61 catches in 1999, his second season, the Steelers drafted another receiver, Plaxico Burress, in the first round of the next draft.

So Ward put the chip on his shoulder and dug in. He battled for playing time in 2000 and caught 48 passes, but then his career took off. Starting in 2001, Ward caught 94, then 112, then 95, and then 80 passes. His production dipped to 69 catches in 2005, but he earned the respect he craved by winning the MVP trophy in Super Bowl XL.

Six years later, Ward is taking 954 receptions for 11,702 yards and 83 touchdowns into the 2011 season. With his 88 playoff catches, he has over 1,000 total receptions.

But how much does Ol' Yeller have left in the tank?

"I have no idea," Ward said. "Do I want to practice and go through training camp again? Right now, I'm just playing game by game, year by year, and I'm blessed to be able to leave this game when I want to leave. If I want to leave right now, I've over-exceeded any expectation by anyone, even myself. I didn't think I'd still be playing in this league, and meanwhile I just found out I moved into 10th all-time in catches. That's crazy. And all the guys on the list didn't take near the same path I did. I wasn't a first-round guy. I wasn't in a passing scheme.

"That, being top 10, kind of validated everything: Like wow, all the hard work, still putting out. For years I used to get caught up in stats, but the years we won Super Bowls I didn't have near the stats I had in years we didn't."

What's the key to his fountain of youth?

"I take care of myself and coach Tomlin doesn't kill me," he said. "I still make some huge crushing blocks, so I haven't lost my edge. And I know this organization. They wouldn't have given me a three-year extension (in 2009) if they thought I was falling.

"I'm all about winning and team and doing my job. The coaches still have faith in me to go out there and get it done. Coach Tomlin calls me Ol' Yeller, as in Mr. Dependable, but I don't like it in the end because Ol' Yeller dies."

But Ol' Yeller can't dance. Tell 'em that, too, Hines.

ACKNOWLEDGMENTS

Truett Smith went ashore in Okinawa with the first wave of American troops in World War II, and he kept going. Word is Smith wandered far inland and, when he wasn't found, was declared Missing in Action. They held a funeral for Smith in his hometown of McComb, Mississippi, where he was grieved by his wife and family. And then he showed up many months later, telling tales of hooking on with a rag-tag army outfit that worked for quarters and food. A short time later, Smith became a single-wing quarterback for the Steelers, proving that even the un-dead could play for the club back in 1950.

I only bring this up because it's a tale that needed to be told, and it's also an example of getting a second chance to appreciate your family. So in my second book, I'd like to first thank my wife, Lydia, for her help in all of this insanity. I also thank our daughter, Samantha, for being the prettiest, smartest, and bestest six-year-old in the whole world. I also thank my parents, Karen and Ken McDonough, for their love and support and for always being there.

As mentioned earlier, this book was inspired by Matthew Cenkner. A promise was made to his mother, Leslie, that the book would be dedicated in his memory. Because of that promise I had no choice but to plow through the difficult times; therefore, this book became Matthew's creation.

I'd also like to thank the former players who returned calls and shared their time. Merril Hoge said he enjoyed his job because of all the brilliant people he talks to every day. I felt the same way talking to these former Steelers. Special thanks to Jack Lambert, who not only agreed to a rare interview but provided inspirational encouragement as well. To all those who returned calls, thank you. To Ray Mathews and Lynn Swann, who called back to decline interviews, thank you as well.

To those who did not respond—Mel Blount, Franco Harris, Tom Keating, John Stallworth, Bennie Cunningham, Mark Malone, Walter Abercrombie, Greg Lloyd, Neil O'Donnell, Jason Gildon, Yancey Thigpen, and Jerome Bettis—maybe next time. And to those I couldn't locate—Ernie Holmes, Dave Smith, Ron Johnson, Cliff Stoudt, Hardy Nickerson, and Andre Hastings—you win the Truett Smith Award.

In paring down the roster for this book, I left out interesting players such as Andy Russell, Terry Bradshaw, and Rocky Bleier because they've written their own books. And I ruled out former players such as Jack Ham, Dwight White, Mike Wagner, L.C. Greenwood, Randy Grossman, and several others who helped me with my previous book *Tales From Behind the Steel Curtain.* The only exception is Joe Greene, who finally won One for the Thumb and remarked on its significance, or lack thereof.

I'd also like to thank the following for their help: Joe Gordon, Bill Priatko, Bob Labriola, Ed Bouchette, Chuck Klausing, Dave Lockett, Vicky Iuni, Mike Fabus, Bob McCartney, Phil Kriedler, Dale Lolley, Donny Drummond, Jim Russell, Bob McLaughlin, Bill Shissler, Patrick Pantano, Bob Carroll, and the many writers over the years whose nuggets of information are now being read by a new generation.